Summers in St. Andrews

ST CROIX RIVER.
Separating Maine from New Brunswick.

PASSAMAQUODDY BAY.
17 MILES LONG.

St. Andrews,
NEW BRUNSWICK.
The ideal Sea-Side Resort
and Health Elysium

Bert Poole — 1896 —

St. Andrews N.B.
AND PASSAMAQUODDY BAY,
FROM "THE ALGONQUIN" HOTEL.

Summers in
St. Andrews

❧ Canada's Idyllic Seaside Resort

WILLA WALKER

First published as *No Hay Fever & A Railway:*
Summers in St. Andrews, Canada's First Seaside Resort

First published as *No Hay Fever & A Railway: Summers in St. Andrews, Canada's First Seaside Resort* by Goose Lane Editions, 1989.
Edited by Rebecca Leaman.
Cover and interior design by Julie Scriver.
Front cover: *High Diving at Katy's Cove* (CPR) (Note: image is shown in reverse)
Back cover: Willa Walker, 1961 (private collection); cover of *No Hay Fever & A Railway: Summers in St. Andrews, Canada's First Seaside Resort*, illustrated by Jennie Lynn-Parish.
Printed in Canada.
10 9 8 7 6 5 4 3 2 1

Library and Archives Canada Cataloguing in Publication

Walker, Willa, 1913-
    Summers in St. Andrews: Canada's idyllic seaside resort / Willa Walker. — Rev. ed.

Previously published under title: No hay fever & a railway: summers in St. Andrews, Canada's first seaside resort.
Includes index.
ISBN 0-86492-456-9

    1. Saint Andrews (N.B.) — History. 2. Saint Andrews (N.B.) — Biography.
3. Vacation homes — New Brunswick — Saint Andrews — History. I. Title.

FC2499.S35W36 2006   971.5'33   C2006-900483-8

Goose Lane Editions acknowledges the financial support of the Canada Council for the Arts, the Government of Canada through the Book Publishing Industry Development Program (BPIDP), and the New Brunswick Department of Wellness, Culture and Sport for its publishing activities.

Goose Lane Editions
330 - 500 Beaverbrook Court
Fredericton, New Brunswick
CANADA E3B 5X4
www.gooselane.com

Contents

Preface

Willa Walker wrote this book about the summer life of St. Andrews when she was seventy-six years old, and she was delighted with how well her work was received. She is now ninety-three, and our family shares her pleasure in this slightly revised edition that remains respectful of her lively original work.

To read our mother's writing is to hear her talk. The style is chatty, and she is charmingly diverted by peoples' foibles and eccentricities. Readers will quickly discover her strong likes and dislikes about the various players. Above all she enjoyed telling people's stories — from the fiery Sir William Van Horne, the builder of the C.P.R., to Thomasina Andrews, the pioneering woman mariner, to C.D. Howe, Canada's minister of war production in World War Two. As she notes, "The town entered their lives, calming the tensions of modern life; it was a place of which to dream, when winter stalked the land."

Willa Walker portrays the lives of the summer people in affectionate detail, but she also reveals her strong social conscience. She writes that she "blushed to recall" that the Katy's Cove beach was closed to townspeople in the morning hours, so the summer people could swim undisturbed. She speaks wistfully of how in her childhood it was the boys, not the girls, who got to ride up front with the McQuoid brothers on their way to picnics in their motorized buckboard. In her Finale to the book she pays tribute "to the real people of St. Andrews" who live all year round in a town where "people are judged on their merits and not by their worldly goods."

Humour is a great unifier that has served summer and year-long residents of St. Andrews very well. We urge readers to sample her stories about the bad-tempered pet mongoose that escaped from its mistress, the great ballroom dancer Irene Castle, and was recaptured by the hotel manager who sought Mrs. Castle's affections; the nanny who told her charges she would have their "guts for garters" if they disobeyed her again; or the elegant ladies who would go for a picnic and a sail aboard a landlocked boat on Deer Island.

There is also great romance to be found, whether it was the young people departing with their sweethearts on the train from St. Andrews station to the Bar Road stop "before dis-embarking and trudging the lonely two miles back to St. Andrews" or the great American composer Irving Berlin, who was refused permission to marry Ellin Mackay by her father because Berlin was Jewish. True to his love, Berlin courted Ellin in St. Andrews and waited for her when she was sent into exile abroad. They eventually married and lived a long and happy life together.

Willa Walker's sons — Giles, Barclay, David, and Julian — are very pleased that her book now returns so boldly to the scene. We thank Goose Lane Editions of Fredericton, notably Susanne Alexander, publisher; Julie Scriver, art director; and editors Rebecca Leaman, Angela Williams, and Laurel Boone, for their dedicated work. We also thank Charlotte McAdam of the Charlotte County Archives for her tireless assistance. We have followed the advice of Goose Lane in changing the name of the book to *Summers in St. Andrews* from the original title *No Hay Fever & A Railway*. Readers delighted in the original title, as we did, but it proved difficult for many to remember in this fast-changing and hurried world.

And lastly, we invite readers to share the excitement that our mother felt each June with the coming of summer in St. Andrews. As she wrote, "The Blockhouse was still there. The Greenock Church steeple and the tall water tower of the Algonquin still stood above the town. Another summer had begun."

Julian H. Walker, March 2006

Opposite: Capt. Rigby and guest sailing on Passamaquoddy Bay. Charlotte County Archives

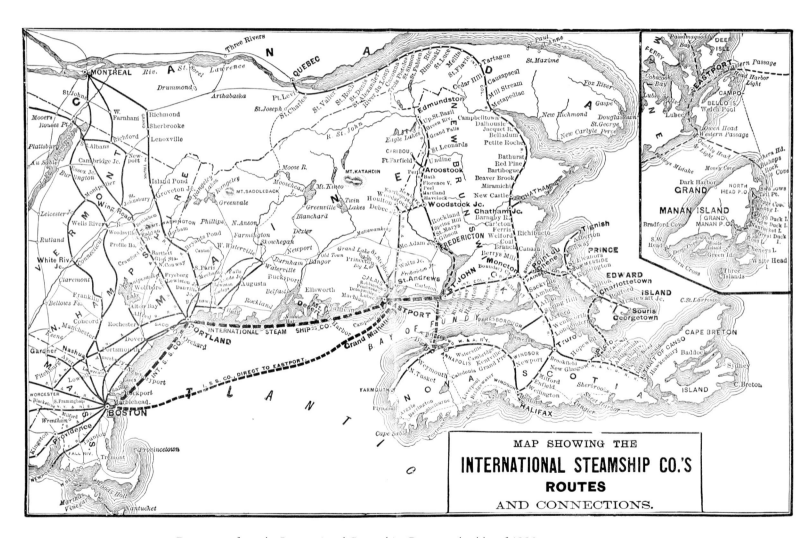

Route map from the International Steamship Company booklet of 1880. Ross Memorial Museum

Preamble

Visitors and tourists have come to St. Andrews from the town's earliest days. The *Standard*, a local newspaper, reported on May 13, 1851, concerning tourists and improvements to St. Andrews: "A pure atmosphere and admirable bathing facilities render it a delightful resort." But how and why did it become one of the most popular summer resorts in eastern Canada and also attract many visitors from the United States?

Apart from its attractive location on Passamaquoddy Bay and its charming houses and gardens, it was a refuge from "hay fever" — which nowadays would be translated into various allergies. Posters and advertisements as early as 1870 proclaimed "No Hay Fever," while the *Argyll* and *Algonquin* hotels printed this claim on their brochures. Before antihistamines people suffered terribly. They were willing to travel long distances to the clean air of the countryside, especially to the seacoast.

In 1871, the *Standard* recorded that several distinguished visitors were staying in town and the *Globe* of Saint John proclaimed that St. Andrews had become the "Watering Place of the Dominion."

One of these distinguished visitors was Sir Leonard Tilley, Minister of Customs. He was the first visitor to own a summer cottage, having bought *Linden Grange* in 1871 from Benjamin Stevenson. (It was later purchased by Miss Olive Hosmer, then owned by the Heenan family of Montreal.) Another visitor at this time was the federal M.P., Dr. Charles — later Sir Charles — Tupper, who in 1872 bought a small stone house on the future site of *Clibrig*, the Wilson estate. With the prestige they acquired as Fathers of Confederation, and

ST. ANDREWS, N.B.

A glance at the accompanying map shows St. Andrews to be situated on a peninsula five miles in length, extending into Passamaquoddy Bay, which is seventeen miles long by six in width, and in point of attraction has but few rivals, with strong points in common and being often compared with the Bay of Naples.

The outer edge of the bay is encircled by mountainous island ranges, which serve to guard both the bay and peninsula from the objectionable fogs of the eastern coast. During the summer months cool breezes prevail, the thermometer seldom reaching 85 degrees Fahrenheit. The town lies on a gentle slope, rising to an altitude of 150 feet in a distance of 2,000 feet from high-water mark. Beyond the town, and for a distance of two miles, sloping hills, attaining 250 feet in height, form an amphitheatre overlooking the town, St. Croix River, coast of Maine, and island-studded bay.

The entire vicinity is traversed by the finest roads. Salt and fresh water fishing is had within an hour's sail or ride, while the bay and lakes afford unsurpassed yachting and boating facilities.

The entire absence of mosquitoes and malaria, the general air of restfulness, together with the curative properties of the balsam-laden atmosphere, have made St. Andrews long and extensively known as an elysium for the hay-fever patient, jaded tourist, pleasure-seeker and sportsman.

The town, of 1700 population, numerous hotels and boarding-houses, has five excellent churches, schools, livery-stables, stores, markets, telegraph office, and a weekly newspaper, "The St. Andrews Beacon," while yachts in charge of reliable captains, canoes with or without their Indian owners, and row-boats can be hired on very reasonable terms.

Advertising poster for the Argyll Hotel.
Charlotte County Archives

by their genuine interest in St. Andrews, Sir Leonard Tilley and Sir Charles Tupper attracted others to the town.

There was a definite local feeling that something should be done about the tourist business and that more hotel rooms were needed. Apart from a few boarding houses, there were two hotels in the town, the *Kennedy Hotel* and the *American House*, but they were small and considered too old. A group of the town's leading citizens formed the St. Andrews Hotel Company in 1871. Its two most important members were Benjamin Stevenson, a lawyer, who later joined the provincial cabinet and became Surveyor General of New Brunswick, and Henry Osburn, an Englishman, who had arrived at St. Andrews in 1860 and was manager of the New Brunswick and Canada Railway. He was also a town councillor. The company decided to build a large new hotel and bought the Eastern Commons, now Indian Point, for that purpose.

The new hotel would be called the *Argyll*. It was built on the northern side of the Eastern Commons, on Ernest Street near the present Community College. However, although digging on the foundation began in 1872, work was long delayed by financial problems. The company raised money by various means. One poster advertised a "Grand Gift Enterprise" to help complete the *Argyll*. Three thousand tickets were to be sold at $5 gold or $5.50 American currency, with a list of prizes in gold or dollars and entry to a Grand Bazaar and Ball at the hotel's opening. But the *Argyll* remained half-finished for nine years until completed in 1881.

Its completion was not without controversy. In 1876, the New Brunswick and Canada Railway, which held charter to provide a daily train service in and out of St. Andrews, decided to cut its service to three trains a week, citing lack of business. A storm of protest followed. The outraged town council and citizens of St. Andrews, led by the postmaster, Fred Campbell, held a meeting and started legal proceedings against the company. But a compromise was reached, largely through the influence of Benjamin Stevenson, a director of the Railway and its legal counsel. The New Brunswick and Canada Railway agreed to finance the completion of the *Argyll Hotel*. Stevenson himself took charge of the work, engaging contractors and even choosing the hotel furnishings.

A BIT OF JOE'S POINT ON THE ST. CROIX ST. ANDREWS N.B.

The opening of the *Argyll* took place on May 24, 1881, Queen Victoria's birthday, with a Grand Ball in the evening. Capt. William Herbert and Mrs. Herbert were the first managers, and the hotel was closed during the winter months. It had capacity for 150 guests and, with a magnificent dining room, had no equal in New Brunswick. A poster depicted the hotel as it was originally planned, not as it was built, since the right wing, over which an American flag floats, was never completed. the *Argyll* appears to have been the first summer hotel on Canada's east coast and in addition to "No Hay Fever" boasted of "Absolute Hay Fever Exemption" in its advertising.

The long delay in building the *Argyll* meant that another new hotel, the reconstructed *Kennedy Hotel* (later the *Shiretown Inn* and then *Kennedy House*), was also opened on May 24, 1881. That first summer season must have been a good one, with 140 people staying at the *Argyll*, 169 at the new *Kennedy Hotel*, and 151 at the *American House*. The latter two were year-round hotels, catering to tourists and business people alike.

Other developments assisted in the steady growth of St. Andrews as a resort town in the late nineteenth century. Early visitors from Central Canada had to make a tortuous and fatiguing journey — from Montreal to Portland on the Grand Trunk Line, which opened in 1853, then by steamer to Eastport on the International Line, and finally by a Frontier Steamboat Company vessel to St. Andrews. But the original optimism of 1871, when the *Argyll* was conceived, had also been fuelled by an event that took place on October 18th of that year south of the border. At Bangor, Maine, President Grant drove the last spike of the Saint John and Maine Railway — making it possible to travel from St. Andrews to Boston in less than twenty-four hours. Though the effects upon the tourist trade were not immediate, the connection would be important.

Robert Gardiner of Boston, a summer visitor from 1879, saw the potential of the town. While the *Argyll* and the St. Andrews Hotel Company still struggled for existence, Gardiner formed a new company, the St. Andrews Land Company, made up of eleven Americans and three Canadians (including members of the St. Andrews Hotel Company board). Sir Leonard

---

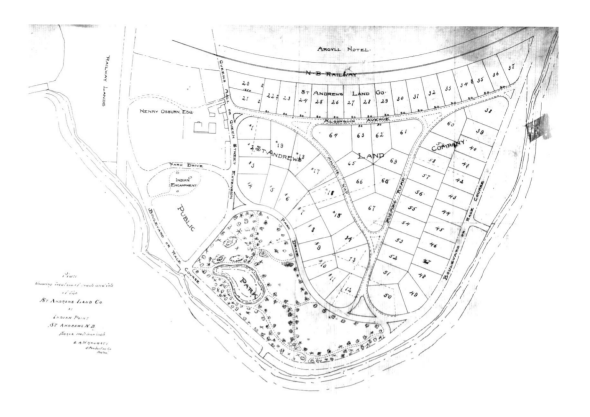

Tilley was president and Gardiner vice-president. The Americans came from Boston and from Portland and Bangor, Maine. Both steamship and railway interests were represented on the St. Andrews Land Company board.

The new company then took over the assets of the St. Andrews Hotel Company, with the exception of the *Argyll*, which was sold to the New Brunswick and Canada Railway. The Land Company proposed to divide the Eastern Commons into sixty building lots and erect cottages, which the company would supply with electricity and water. Yet this never happened; indeed, only one cottage was ever built. It was called the *Queen Anne* or *Park Cottage*. In 1890 it was moved to the corner of Elizabeth and Carleton streets, where it was then named *Algonquin Cottage* and advertised for sale or rent by the Land Company. In 1900 it was bought by David R. Forgan, a Scotsman and banker. Extensive alterations and additions were made by later owners, particularly by Mr. and Mrs. John Cowans.

A racetrack or boulevard ran along the shore of the peninsula at the Eastern Commons (Indian Point). Carriages used it and sometimes there were race meetings. Behind this a park was laid out with shrubs, trees, and an artificial lake. The Land Company also purchased a great deal more land until it owned most of Barrack Hill, now Prince of Wales Street, and many acres along Joe's Point Road and elsewhere.

One of the Land Company's major contributions to the town was the establishment of the Chamcook Water Company, whose object was to supply water from Chamcook Lake to residents. But many residents felt that expenditure on improved water supplies was not warranted. In 1889 the *Beacon* claimed that "there was an abundance of good water from wells for domestic purposes and an ample supply for fire protection." At the same time there were reports of impure wells and even a recent death from bad water. After a great deal of anxious talk, however, and many visits to the Legislature in Fredericton, St. Andrews received its new water supply.

By 1889 the St. Andrews Land Company was doing so much business that it built a red brick office on Water Street, while also maintaining an office in Boston. F. Howard Grimmer was the first company secretary, followed by Frank Mallory. In truth, the Land Company's advertising paid off; on several occasions newspapermen and influential visitors were brought to St. Andrews on special trains. Although the Eastern Commons development failed, many other fine lots were sold and the company had acquired the land where the *Algonquin Hotel* was to be built. The Land Company redeemed the town's fortunes. Some years earlier, when the New Brunswick and Canada Railway reduced passenger service to the town, F.W. Cram, the general manager, stated that the lack of traffic was such that it did not justify repairing the bad road and tracks. A decade later things were very different. Well-to-do visitors were building on the new lots. The *Argyll* was flourishing, with a railway stop in its own grounds and a steamship wharf within three minutes walk. *Kennedy*'s was also thriving.

Indeed, 1889 was the great year for the town of St. Andrews. As a result of long negotiations with the Canadian Pacific Railway, the first train arrived in St. Andrews over C.P.R. tracks on June 3, 1889, and the *Algonquin Hotel*, financed and built by the Algonquin Hotel Company, opened on July 1st. The *Algonquin* would give St. Andrews an elegant centre for a summer society blessed with No Hay Fever — and a Railway.

Rendering of the Algonquin Cottage, property of F. Howard Grimmer

Charlotte County Archives

The Algonquin Hotel

The *Algonquin* opened its doors on July 1, 1889, under the management of Fred A. Jones of Saint John. A well-publicized grand opening, three days earlier, was attended by many important guests from New Brunswick, Maine, and Massachusetts. A Pullman car excursion from Boston brought many of the visitors while other special Pullmans brought the V.I.P. guests, such as the Governor General of Canada, Lord Stanley, the Governor of Maine, Edwin C. Burleigh, and the Lieutenant-Governor of Ontario, Alexander Campbell.

The steam yacht of the St. Andrews Land Company was at anchor the day of the opening to take the official guests on excursions, and dinners and receptions were held.

The Prime Minister, Sir John A. Macdonald, and Lady Macdonald stayed at the *Algonquin* soon after it opened. Visitors could now travel from Montreal on the C.P.R. and from New England on the Boston and Maine Railroad — by day or overnight in well-appointed Pullman

The first Algonquin Hotel, built in 1889.
D. Will McKay

Opposite: Cover of the original brochure advertising the Algonquin Hotel, 1894.
Private Collection

cars. The steamers of the International Line would bring passengers from Saint John, Boston, and Portland. Those from Portland sailed to Eastport, Maine, where the smaller vessels of the Frontier Steamboat Company connected for St. Andrews. There was a Customs House in the town, and an officer met the steamers at the wharf.

Fine photographs of the first *Algonquin Hotel* still exist, and, perhaps best of all, the official brochure for 1889 is in the Charlotte County Archives (together with several later brochures). "No Hay Fever" was again printed in large type on all the hotel's advertising, which also claimed that mosquitoes were unknown in St. Andrews.

The hotel was designed by the architects Rand and Taylor of Boston, and built of wood. It had a long, open verandah with a commanding view overlooking the harbour. There were eighty-five bedrooms and an elevator — a convenience not possessed by any other eastern summer hotel — while a novelty was provided in the form of optional salt or fresh-water baths. The rooms were priced between three and five dollars per day; weekly rates ran from twelve dollars upwards.

At the time the *Algonquin* was being built, Robert Gardiner bought "Samson Spring." This source of special water, thought to have medicinal value, was situated on the Cemetery Road (where it branches down to the bathing beach). Water was hauled daily from the spring to the hotel dining room, while bellboys carried individual orders to the guests' rooms. Many bottles were also shipped home.

"Samson Spring" was later taken over by the hotel. Charles Horsnell, who would do all the stone work for Sir William Van Horne's estate — the walls, cement flower pots along the driveway to *Covenhoven*, the circular bathhouse, etc. — also bricked up the spring and constructed seats there for the use of hotel guests.

The *Algonquin*'s advertising material contained vivid descriptions of the lakes and streams available for trout and salmon fishing, accompanied by an Indian guide. There was canoeing; there were yachts for sailing, and schooners for trips to the islands or for picnics and deep-sea fishing on Passamaquoddy Bay. Croquet, tennis, and a green for bowls (on the lawn in front of the hotel) were also available. Ladies in their long dresses and large hats participated in all these sports, and later on they became enthusiastic golfers when the golf course opened in 1894.

Those were happy and carefree days, with carriages and saddle horses for hire and lovely drives along the seacoast with no traffic. Around the town the dirt roads were sprayed with water to keep down the dust and protect the ladies' and gentlemen's clothes.

UNDER MINISTERS ISLAND ST. ANDREWS. N.B.

From two of the early *Algonquin* ledgers, one for 1891-1893 and the other for 1895, we can examine lists of guests, where they came from, and the prices they paid for their rooms, for picnic lunches, laundry, baths, carriages, and so on. When the *Algonquin* opened in 1889, almost all the early guests were American. They came from Boston, New York, Texas, Kalamazoo, New Jersey, Rhode Island, Baltimore, Iowa, Minneapolis, Washington, D.C., Missouri, and elsewhere. The few Canadian guests came from Montreal, Toronto, and Ottawa, and there were very few from Saint John, Fredericton, and elsewhere in the Maritimes.

One of the first guests from Saint John was Mrs. George F. Smith, a widow, with her three young daughters, aged eight, ten, and twelve — Leslie (Bebe), Amy, and Constance. They came on July 28, 1892, and the price for the four of them for one week, with meals, was $60. The only other Saint John names from that time were those of Mr. and Mrs. H. Fairweather.

Frequent guests from Montreal in those early days were the Bigelows, Cantlies, Drummonds, Robert Meighens, J.B. Wheelers, Campbell-Nelleses, and Redpaths, while the following Montreal guests all built summer cottages later on: the Hopes, Hosmers, F. W. Thompsons, Van Hornes, and Shaughnessys. The only Ottawa family mentioned in 1895 was that of Mrs. W.K. Rowley and her sons.

Many early visitors were to return and strengthen their connection with St. Andrews. Mr. and Mrs. Gorham Hubbard Sr. of Boston were guests at the *Algonquin* in 1893; their granddaughter and her husband became residents of St. Andrews. Mr. Robert Gardiner and his family, also of Boston, were frequent guests during 1892, before he built his cottage the following year. His grandson, Robert Payne, for many years had a house in St. Andrews called the *Anchorage*.

Mrs. C.J. Bonaparte and her son, Charles Bonaparte, from Baltimore, came in July 1891 and visited frequently over the years. Charles Bonaparte was a grandnephew of Emperor Napoleon I and grandson of Jerome Bonaparte, who married Betsy Patterson of Baltimore. He was long remembered by the people in St. Andrews because he always carried a white umbrella, rain or shine. One report in an old scrapbook says that Charles came to the town for twenty-four summers, which is correct, and asserts that Bonaparte Lake was named after him — but this has not been confirmed.

The *Algonquin* became even more important to St. Andrews when the *Argyll* burned to the ground in 1892, leaving the town with a single major hotel. The *St. Andrews Beacon* of March 24, 1892, reported the event fully:

The Lessons of the Late Fire

In the present deprived state of business in St. Andrews, the destruction of The Argyll Hotel cannot be regarded by sensible people in any other light than as a serious loss to the town. Yet the people of the town have nobody to blame for the disaster but themselves. A little water, judiciously applied, could easily have subdued the flames before they had obtained control of the building, but the water was not to be had, so the building was destroyed. Even had there been an abundance of water at hand, it is extremely doubtful if it could have been used to advantage by the antiquated fire extinguishing apparatus which the town possesses. The fault does not lie with the firemen. They did all that it was possible for men to do to get the heavy machines to the fire promptly, but the task was a most exhausting one, and they were not to blame if they had to stop for a minute or two for rest. The time that was thus consumed decided the fate of the building. The lessons to be taken from this fire are obvious – first, that the town needs a better water service. Secondly, that it needs better apparatus for the extinguishment of fire than it now possesses.

St. Andrews Beacon,
March 24, 1892

The *Argyll Hotel* — the pioneer summer hotel of St. Andrews — was reduced from a stately structure to a pile of smouldering ashes, on Sunday evening last.

After the closing of the hotel season, last year, Mrs. Herbert, widow of the former proprietor, went to the United States for the winter months, leaving the house in charge of Mr. and Mrs. W.H. Williamson. They were careful people, and everything went well about the house until Sunday last.

About 1 o'clock that day a fire was lighted in the gentlemen's parlour, a large room in the ground floor to the right of the main entrance. A fire was kept alive in the fireplace all the afternoon, without anything occurring to arouse the suspicions of the inmates of the house. As Mrs. Williamson sat down to tea, in one of the rooms a short distance from where the fire was burning, she heard a noise as if two doors had slammed together. Going out to ascertain the cause she smelled a strong smell of smoke.

Strong Smell of Smoke

There was a little smoke visible in the gentlemen's parlour, but nothing of any consequence. Going upstairs to the second floor, she threw open the doors of the ladies' parlour (which was located just over the other parlour), and a thick cloud of smoke thrust itself in her face. Thoroughly alarmed, she seized a dinner bell, and ran to the residence of Mr. Thos. Armstrong, about 250 yards distant. As quickly as possible a general alarm was given. After alarming the neighbours, Mrs. Williamson flew back to the hotel, and running upstairs again, groped her way through the blinding smoke in the ladies' parlour to obtain possession of a box belonging to her which contained valuable papers. She found the box, and when she was coming out of the room the flames were making themselves manifest through the hall floor on the second flat.

Although the firemen made a quick response to the alarm, it took them almost 20 minutes to drag the lumbering old machines, honoured by the name of fire-engines, to the scene of the fire. When they got there, there was no water to be had nearer than in a well across the track, alongside the railway tank, and another in the rear of the Land Company's Cottage. What seemed an hour was consumed in getting connections made. By this time, the fire was burning fiercely alongside the chimney on the three floors, and the blinding smoke made it almost impossible for men to live on the inside. They stayed and fought the flames for about half an hour, when the water gave out, and they were reluctantly forced to give up the struggle.

In the meantime, scores of willing hands in various parts of the house were engaged in removing the furniture. All the furniture on the lower floor was taken out. On the second floor, with the exception of two or three rooms, which were so full of smoke that nobody could stay in them a minute, nearly all the rooms were emptied of their contents. Some furniture was also taken out of the 4th floor, the men working in the rooms until the approaching fire compelled them to lower themselves to the ground by means of ropes. There were 14 rooms in the second floor of the ell, over the dining hall and billiard room, and they were all divested of their contents before the flames took

The Argyll Hotel. Built in 1881, it was destroyed by fire in 1892. D. Will McKay

possession. The upper floor of the ell did not fare so well, very few things being rescued. An organ belonging to one of the last season's guests was taken out in a slightly damaged state, but the hotel piano was almost ruined before a rescue was effected.

Given Over to the Flames

When the firemen deserted the building the southern portion of it was a mass of fiercely burning flames. There was a strong northwest wind blowing, which, while helping to feed the fire, also retarded its progress in the northern half of the building. But, inch by inch, it increased its fiery grasp, until at 8 o'clock the entire building was in a seething, roaring flame. It was a magnificent sight, but the majority of the spectators were too full of regret at the destruction of the house to appreciate the grandeur before them. The front chimney, which had no doubt been the cause of the conflagration, fell about 8:30 o'clock, the bricks being scattered far out amongst the crowd. No one was injured, though some people had very narrow escapes. All the other chimneys, with the exception of one leading from the main dining room, fell as the woodwork was burned away from them. The latter maintained its erect attitude until the following morning, when it was thrown down to prevent its descending on the heads of those standing about.

A lady golfer at St. Andrews, c. 1905. Private Collection

The Fire Became Spent

It was after midnight before the fire had exhausted itself. After that time all that was standing of the once handsome *Argyll Hotel* were the chimney above-mentioned, two or three other pieces of brickwork, and an outhouse, which had been attached to the main building by a covered passage-way, familiarly termed the "bridge of sighs." This building was burned, but the small building was unscathed. The barn and its contents escaped.

The Insurance

There was very little insurance on the building or its contents. The Western and British America held policies on the building for $6,000, which just covered outstanding mortgages. On the furniture, most of which was saved in a damaged state, there was insurance of $1,000 in the North British and Mercantile Office. The total loss is estimated at $15,000.

Incidents of the Fire

The furniture, which was removed from the hotel, was left out all night in the fields, a guard being placed over it by the insurance agents.

The Land Company's *Cottage in the Park* was in imminent danger of destruction, but by careful watching, its destruction was prevented.

John Rooney had his head injured by a chair being thrown upon it from the third storey.

St. Andrews Beacon, March 24, 1892

Undaunted by the fire, in 1894 the St. Andrews Land Company undertook another project — the design and building of a golf course. There were very few courses at that time in eastern Canada, and the venture caused interest far and wide. It came about mainly through the efforts of Robert S. Gardiner, vice-president of the Land Company, who also paid for the construction of the first clubhouse and donated several silver cups for competitions, many of the fine trophies still in use over a century later.

A nine-hole course was laid out on the Peacock pasture, leased for the purpose, just beyond the Peacock house (later the home of Mr. and Mrs. G. Melvin Turner on Joe's Point

Road). Several years later the links were extended to make an eighteen-hole course. Transportation to the golf club was provided by Albert Denley's horse-drawn bus, the fare being five cents. Around 1920 the C.P.R. bought the Almshouse property from the town, and there an additional nine-hole course was made. A new and larger clubhouse was then erected off Reed Avenue.

For some years after the hotel was built there was no telephone service in St. Andrews. A messenger boy employed by Mr. W.E. Mallory, who owned the livery stable, was stationed in the hotel lobby, and when a carriage was needed by one of the guests he would leap upon his bicycle and dash down to Water Street. After delivering the order, he would place his bicycle on the back of the carriage and return to the *Algonquin*.

The first clubhouse for the Algonquin golf course, built by Robert S. Gardiner in 1893. Private Collection

But all that changed in 1900 when Mr. Mallory installed a private telephone line between his stable and the hotel. Later that same year he persuaded Sir William Van Horne to have a line installed between Minister's Island and the C.P.R. railway station. It was not until 1903, though, that St. Andrews received its first town telephone service. The switchboard was in Mr. Howard Rigby's house, and his daughter Madge was the first operator. There were less than thirty subscribers at the time.

Meanwhile, the *Algonquin Hotel* had every appearance of prosperity. In 1902, however, it ran into financial difficulties and was sold to the C.P.R., which took over its management. This heralded a new era for St. Andrews, possessing one of the great C.P.R. hotels, which had already made their reputation for excellence. *Banff Springs Hotel* and the *Hotel Vancouver* had been built in 1888; the *Chateau Frontenac* in Quebec and the *Place Viger Hotel* in Montreal in 1893; the *Royal Alexandra* in Winnipeg in 1904. *Chateau Lake Louise* and the *Empress* in Victoria followed in 1908. Prior to purchasing the *Algonquin* in 1905, the only hotel the C.P.R. owned east of Quebec was the *Station Hotel* in McAdam, New Brunswick, built in 1901.

As part of the C.P.R. chain, the *Algonquin* gained the benefits of a vigorous advertising campaign across Canada. Well-known artists were employed to paint pictures of the C.P.R. hotels and design some of their posters. G. Horne Russell was one of these artists, and he later

THE ALGONQUIN HOTEL BURNED TO THE GROUND
PROPERTY VALUED AT THREE QUARTERS OF A MILLION DOLLARS
MADE SPECTACULAR BLAZE AT ST. ANDREWS ON SATURDAY

If it were not for the concrete additions which were made in recent years, there would be nothing left of the stately Algonquin Hotel today but a heap of smouldering ruins. Every atom of woodwork about the great building, including the central section, the roofs of the concrete wings, the wooden stairways and partitions, etc., was completely destroyed in the fire which began at noon on Saturday, and raged throughout the afternoon.

The fire originated from a charcoal spark which had gone beneath the shingles on the northeast concrete wing, while some repairs were being made by workmen. Smouldering on the tarred paper it worked its way to the woodwork while the men were at dinner, and a great conflagration was the result.

The water supply which had been turned off for the winter had not been restored, so that there was little to fight the fire with except buckets. In less than an hour after the fire started, fanned by a westerly gale, the flames had eaten through to the four storey central section of wood. Being highly inflammable it burned with great fierceness, the sparks being carried miles away. Some of them even set fire to the grass alongside Sir William Van Horne's summer house on Minister's Island. George Chase's farm buildings a mile away were fired by these windblown sparks, but the fire was speedily extinguished.

Half an hour after the flames had taken hold of the wooden section it was completely destroyed together with the board verandahs in front. Then the fire penetrated the western concrete wing which was built two years ago. Everything of an inflammable nature in its five storeys was burned. It was feared that the explosion of the ammonia tanks near the refrigerator would result in possible accident to human life, but happily this did not occur. The fire burned in this section like a great furnace for several hours. . . . There were many beautiful summer cottages within the fire zone, but with the exception of No. 1 Algonquin cottage, which stood immediately to the north of the hotel, all the cottages were saved. The summer cottage of George B. Hopkins, of New York, which was separated from the hotel by only the width of the street was on fire several times but the firemen by desperate efforts succeeded in saving it. Had it burned, the summer houses of Mr. Gill, of Ottawa, Mr. Southam, of Ottawa, Mr. Seeley, of Montreal, Prof. Smith, of Cambridge, and possibly the summer residence of Sir Thomas Shaughnessy would have been destroyed. Nearly all the interior furnishings on the lower floor of the hotel were taken out before the fire reached it and were safely removed to the casino, but with this exception little of the contents of the hotel were saved. . . .

Saint Croix Courier, April 16, 1914

Above and opposite: the Algonquin fire, April 15, 1914. D. Will McKay

built his own summer cottage in St. Andrews. A period of success and expansion followed for St. Andrews as a seaside resort. A new wing was added to the hotel in 1908 and another in 1912. Meanwhile, more and more cottages were occupied. Those summers before the First World War seemed to stretch out in leisurely confidence, typified by the *Algonquin*'s elegant, unhurried style.

Then suddenly, and perhaps prophetically, the lovely hotel that gave the town so much of its character was destroyed by fire like the *Argyll* before it. The fire of April 11, 1914, must have seemed devastating to the summer economy of St. Andrews. Despite wartime difficulties a new *Algonquin* was built the very next year, this time out of poured cement, designed by Mr. Ernest Barott of Montreal. The rebuilding came about largely through the influence of Sir William Van Horne and Lord Shaughnessy.

Now relatively fireproof, the *Algonquin* could also offer many new facilities, with accommodations for 250 guests. Ninety-seven rooms had private baths and twenty-two rooms had private lavatories. (In 1950, Peter Barott, Ernest's son and also an architect, was outraged to

The Algonquin Hotel. C.P.R.

find that he had to share a bathroom at the *Algonquin*.) There was a children's dining room and also a very cosy smoking room.

The interior decorating of the hotel was done by Kate Reed (Mrs. Hayter Reed). When her husband was appointed manger-in-chief of the C.P.R. Hotel Department by Lord Shaughnessy in 1905, Kate Reed became head of the Furnishing Department. She was both knowledgeable and artistic, with a flair for blending just the right colours and making the interior of each hotel unique and charming. At the *Algonquin* there were wicker chairs, sofas, and tables in the large lounge, with pretty, bright-coloured chintz cushions and long curtains. Each bedroom was furnished with pale summery furniture. As the hotel's brochure declared, it was a "delight to behold."

And Kate Reed's trademark was evident at the *Algonquin*, with mottoes, quotations, or verses painted above fireplaces or on the backs of benches. They were also used in *The Inn*, which the C.P.R. owned, but especially in the Reed's own house, *Pansy Patch*, which they built in 1912 on Carleton Street just below the *Algonquin*.

Guests now often came for long periods of time, a month or six weeks, and they sometimes furnished their own suites. They had their own cars and chauffeurs, and saddle horses that they stabled in a barn on Montague Street. Regular guests returned summer after summer, and British names were added to those of eminent Canadian and American guests after the C.P. Steamship Line was established. Every Governor General of Canada during this period visited the *Algonquin* at one time or another.

There were also five hotel cottages that were rented each summer, usually by the same families. Four were built between 1904 and 1907, in close proximity to the hotel on Prince of Wales Street. After Number 1 burned down in 1914 — when the hotel itself was destroyed — the numbers of the others were never changed. This sometimes caused confusion for strangers. The largest cottage (Number 5) was an old converted house situated at the back door of the hotel. It was used by the manager and his family.

Mr. J.M. Plaut and his wife, Alice Sachs Plaut, from Cincinnati, came to the cottages with their two children in 1915-1916. They did not return until the late 1940s, renting Number 3 for twenty-five years. Other long-time *Algonquin* cottage residents were the Henry Joseph family from Montreal, the Douglas Cowans family, and Mr. and Mrs. Norman Armour of New York City.

Of course, the *Algonquin* guests and those people staying at summer cottages were part of the same society. Dinner parties were given at the cottages and the hotels, and most summer visitors met at the dances at the Casino.

The Casino was one of the special features of the *Algonquin*, built in 1913 before the fire. It was situated directly opposite the hotel, overlooking the tennis courts, and had wide covered verandahs. In the basement of the Casino were three bowling alleys and a splendid billiard room with numerous tables. Upstairs, the large room had a beautiful hardwood floor for dancing. It was used for many social functions and later as a cinema.

Katy's Cove had been used for swimming for a long time. But money was now spent to improve it immensely. A dam with sluice gates was built where the train crossed the railway bridge so that the flow of water from the sea could be controlled and the water warmed. New and better bathhouses were then built.

Some recreational needs had to be supplied more discreetly than others. There was Prohibition in New Brunswick until 1927 (when the Liquor Control Board was formed). Indeed, spirits or beer could not be sold in public places until 1962, when Premier Louis Robichaud established the Liquor Licensing Board. In the *Algonquin*, however, there was a dark and private bar below the lobby. One could enter by a stairway inside the hotel or by an outside door. Only milk shakes and soft drinks were sold but guests got round the difficulty by bringing their own bottles. Much later, the powerful C.P.R. defied the law and served drinks without a licence, arguing that otherwise the tourist trade would be hurt.

With the increase in tourism and in the popularity of the *Algonquin*, the C.P.R. concentrated a good deal of advertising on St. Andrews. At some point the town became "St. Andrews-by-the-Sea," a name which appeared on all the C.P.R. brochures and letterhead. This practice was largely followed by summer visitors, who addressed their correspondence that way, but the residents of the town disliked the name. They were proud of St. Andrews unadorned — the name under which the Loyalists had established the town in 1783 — and although the coined name continued to be used by the Chamber of Commerce and in tourist promotion, it is essentially artificial.

Nevertheless, the people of St. Andrews and the C.P.R. have had a close and remarkably good relationship over the years. The hotel and the railway provided a great many jobs for local people, sometimes for all their working lives. The railway has gone now, and the *Algonquin* has changed hands and does not require the staff it once did, but the tradition lives on in vivid memories. During the heyday of the C.P.R.'s great seaside hotel, it was the character of the people, as well as the town's serene physical beauty, which attracted so many to St. Andrews. The town entered their lives, calming the tensions of modern life; it was a place of which to dream when winter stalked the land.

The Kennedy Hotel

Mr. Angus Kennedy came to New Brunswick in 1857. He was a railway contractor, who took a subcontract to lay a section of the New Brunswick and Canada Railway, and then came to St. Andrews. Later on he decided to become an innkeeper, and his first inn was located on Water Street. From there he moved to larger premises near the former railway station, but after several years his hotel was destroyed by fire and he moved uptown to the *American House*. It was at that time he purchased the site upon which he built the new *Kennedy Hotel* on Water Street — known locally thereafter as Kennedy's — which opened on May 24, 1881.

Angus Kennedy was an enterprising proprietor, and with his son Frank as partner the hotel flourished, becoming a centre for social life in the town, where dances and wedding receptions were held. Angus Kennedy died in 1904 but Frank continued to manage the *Kennedy Hotel*,

The Kennedy Hotel, built in 1881, later the Shiretown Inn.

becoming one of the town's outstanding businessmen. He was elected mayor in 1920 and again in 1932-1933. A generous and kindly man, he was remembered affectionately for many years after his death in 1934 at the age of fifty-seven.

His great friend had been Sheriff Charles W. Mallory, a devoted Presbyterian and supporter of the Conservative Party – while Frank Kennedy was a devout Catholic and a Liberal. When Frank Kennedy was considering running for the Legislative Assembly, Sheriff Mallory was heard to say: "If that happens, in spite of voting Conservative all my life, I will have to vote Liberal."

Though the family continued to run the hotel after Frank's death, the hotel was sold in 1946 by Amelia Kennedy, Jennie Owens, and Archibald Kennedy (two sisters and a brother of Frank) to Gerald G. O'Brien of Saint John. Gerry O'Brien changed the name to the *Commodore Hotel* but sold it in 1947 to John Taylor, also from Saint John. "Chokey" Taylor, as he was called, was a tall good-looking man, an outstanding sailor of small yachts, who had a distinguished career in the Second World War on the North Atlantic convoys. Chokey spent so much time away from the *Commodore* that it is difficult to say if he was a good hotelier or not. His ownership lasted until 1961, when he sold out to M.M.S. Ltd.

That was the name of Mr. and Mrs. Ian MacKay's family firm. Ian and Leni MacKay were no strangers to St. Andrews; Ian had worked for the C.P.R. for some time, of which five years were spent at the *Algonquin*. Once again the name of the downtown hotel was changed. The *Commodore* became the *Shiretown Inn*, and many attractive improvements were made, in keeping with the hotel's history. The MacKays also contributed greatly to St. Andrews by buying and restoring several buildings on Water Street opposite the *Shiretown* and converting smaller buildings into attractive apartments.

Opposite: The Kennedy Hotel on Water Street on the occasion of the Duke of Connaught's visit to open Prince Arthur School, c. 1912. Charlotte County Archives

The Inn or Osburn House (Indian Point)

The Inn was built for Julius Thompson, first manager of the New Brunswick and Canada Railway, as his own dwelling. That was about 1851 (the first sod for the Railway was turned in 1852). When Julius Thompson retired he was succeeded as manager by Henry Osburn, the Englishman who had already made a name for himself as a railway builder and engineer. Osburn arrived in 1860, took over the Thompson house, and named it *Kamoosaba*. There he lived until 1888, when he and his family returned to England.

It was a large gabled house with deep wainscotted windows, stables, and a tennis court at one side, a driveway for carriages, and a lovely garden with fine shrubs and trees. It became the possession of F. W. Cram, when he took over the New Brunswick and Canada Railway, until *Kamoosaba* — or *Osburn House* as it was more commonly called — was bought by the C.P.R. in 1907-1908.

Mrs. Allerton, wife of the *Algonquin*'s manager, was caretaker of *Osburn House*, and after it had been refurbished she ran it as a small hotel or annex to the *Algonquin*. The Hayter Reeds renamed it *The Inn*.

People enjoyed staying at *The Inn*. Situated over the railway tracks at Indian Point, it was much less grand than the *Algonquin* and conveniently located close to the wharves, the station, and the beach. Children loved the old house – there was so much room to play in the garden.

Kate Reed was responsible for redecorating *The Inn*, and she and her husband later stayed there from time to time. As manager of all the C.P.R. hotels, Hayter Reed travelled a lot, and Kate had other hotels to decorate, but they had a special affection for *The Inn* even after they built *Pansy Patch* for themselves.

Kate made friends with the Nicholases, a Maliseet family who lived next door. John Nicholas was a well-known guide who had often taken his good friend Henry Osburn hunting and fishing. When Kate Reed arrived in St. Andrews in the spring of 1907, the Osburns were long gone. But a year later she wrote the following letter to them:

Opposite: Hayter and Kate Reed at ease at The Inn, 1908. C.P.R.

The Inn, with guests sunning in the garden, c. 1907-1908. C.P.R.

The Canadian Pacific Railway Company
The Inn
St. Andrews, N.B.
Sunday evening May 24th, 1908

Probably a day of many memories for you all in this dear old house, my dear Mr. & Mrs. Osborne!

I am sitting out in the kitchen, not your old kitchen for that is now the dining room, but the shed converted into a kitchen, & have been listening for the last hour to old Mrs. Nicholas telling interesting stories of you all! How the dear old thing loves you! The tears were in her eyes many times — I have met many interesting characters down here but none half as interesting as she is! Such a sense of humour, the laugh always following the sigh and the tear and such heart! She said she would bring over your address tomorrow.

Last spring when a friend of mine and I came down here to hang curtains and sew rag carpets, we were sitting in the back parlour sewing away, when she said "Kate" — my name is Kate — "Who lived in this house?" I said a family named Osborne, I wish I knew more about them (neither of us had ever been in St. Andrews before). She said looking up and about, as if she saw ghosts, "well I feel they were dear loving hospitable people," and I said, "do you know I feel the same way, it feels like a home, I feel there was much happiness here. I know there must have been a large family, and given to hospitality by the size of the house. As I am the eldest of 11, I know something about large families and big houses!" and so we talked and dreamed back.

I am the wife of Mr. Hayter Reed, who has charge of the C.P.R Hotels and he would tell you if he could only see you, that of all the Hotels, *THE INN* is nearest my heart! Perhaps because I had to work hardest to make it comfortable — the C.P.R. gets very economical at times! — that I had to do everything myself, except weave the rag carpets! I have tried to make it homey and homespunny. One of the mottoes I have put up in the dining room will best tell my feeling. "Hath not old custom made this place more sweet than painted pomp?" My husband and I thought much of what we would call this dear place, as so many people wanted so many difficult names unspellable and unpronounceable, that I said let us decide on something short and easy and call it *THE INN*, and so it is. I painted a sign which hangs over your porch. In one corner is a lighthouse and in another a sail boat and between the two [*The Inn*]. Next year if Sir Thomas [Shaughnessy] feels a little less POOR, we want to make many improvements and make the garden as you used to have it. I know your garden was lovely because Mrs. Vroom, from St. Stephen, said so yesterday. She said how happy she used to be when she was over here as a little girl. Mr. Vroom and I are great friends, as he does so much for *The Algonquin* — I try to be interested in *The Algonquin*, but it isn't in it with this place! I must leave and go back to Montreal to get ready to go West. There is so much to be done out there and my husband, who is in our new hotel in Victoria, is telegraphing me to hurry!

My dear old pen broke just as I was going to say goodnight last night. Mrs. Nicholas has just come in with your address in Mrs. Osburn's dear Christmas letter! Forgive me for spelling your name wrong. I join with her (Mrs. Nicholas) in blessing you all!

Your soul Friend,
Kate Reed

Donated to the Charlotte County Archives by A.G. (Tony) Osburn of Vancouver, Henry Osburn's grandson.

What pleasure it must have given to Mr. and Mrs. Osburn and their five children to receive this warm and charming letter penned in their beloved *Kamoosaba*.

Henry Osburn died in London in 1911 at the age of eighty. Despite its enduring features, such as the tall cedar poles which marked its carriage drive, *The Inn* was used less and less and became derelict. It was torn down in 1932. But perhaps Kate Reed's letter preserves more than a shadow of the affections this house once inspired.

Opposite: Masquerade Ball at the Casino, the Algonquin, 1930. Standing, left to right: Mrs. Alice Wilson; the Hon. Marguerite Shaughnessy; Mrs. Helen Balfour; Howard W. Pillow — with others unidentified. Private Collection

A Vignette

1930

Summers in St. Andrews Between the Wars

St. Andrews was a happy place for children and young people. Families came for two months or more, and those who stayed at the *Algonquin* sometimes furnished their own suites of rooms, bringing personal maids or employing local help: nurses for children or grandchildren, automobiles and chauffeurs, and riding horses.

The summer cottage people brought maids and all their housekeeping requirements. They also had to feed themselves. They bought their groceries at O'Neill's and Doon's, and since there was virtually no tinned food everything was bought in bulk and was packaged by the store — sugar, flour, tea, coffee, everything. The cooks from the bigger houses would give written orders for the day to a young man sent from the grocery store. Then all orders were supposed to be filled and delivered before lunch — a big undertaking. Some ladies would drive to the shops themselves in their carriages, later in their cars, and order their groceries while remaining seated in the vehicle. In due course, huge orders of staples and tinned goods from Eaton's would be sent to the cottages by C.P.R. express from Montreal, Toronto, and Ottawa.

In those days the *Algonquin* was largely a family hotel; there were no bus tours or conventions (except perhaps select groups during the 1930s). Children had their meals in their own dining room, where they had to be dressed properly. As they became familiar with the *Algonquin*, however, they observed its daily customs — for like any large hotel it had its special rules.

There were certain coveted privileges. Peacock Alley, on the verandah part of the dining room, with the best view, was reserved for permanent residents or visitors of importance — it was demeaning to be placed at a table inside the main dining room. Meanwhile, young girls used to sell small bouquets of wild or garden flowers at the hotel. At the beginning, they were only permitted to sit on the side verandah, not on the front steps, but later they sat at the foot of the stairs near the elevator. Many of those girls became worthy matrons of St. Andrews

Opposite: Beach scene at Katy's Cove, c. 1934. C.P.R.

— just as local lawyers, judges, doctors, teachers, and businessmen were former bellboys and waiters.

There was a permanent hairdresser who came summer after summer, as well as a barber-shop and a shoe-cleaning stall. Lawn bowls was played in front of the hotel, and there was croquet across the road from the side door to the old Inness-Hopkins house (which later burned down). The four rather poor clay tennis courts took a very long time to dry after rain, and players had to roll the courts themselves. But there were several other courts at the private cottages, and a lot of tennis was played. George Brown, who played the cello in the orchestra, gave tennis lessons. Well-organized and serious tournaments were held every summer, with large silver cups donated by generous summer visitors — Sir Thomas Tait, R.J. Christie, Thomas J. Clark, William W. Fitler, William M. Garden — in addition to the Magee Memorial Cup.

On wet days, in particular, the Casino was the centre for activities, especially the bowling alley downstairs. The wicker sofas and armchairs were arranged in rows for movies — held several times a week. The acoustics were poor but everyone enjoyed the show. Thursdays and

Saturdays were dance nights, with the hotel orchestra led by Percy Levine playing all the wonderful old dance tunes. Teenage boys and girls shyly learned to ballroom dance; sixteen-year-olds went on their first dates well chaperoned; the middle-aged romped about the dance floor. Later on the pianist was Tom Kelly, who would also play after lunch and in the evenings in the hotel lounge. Since no drinks were served in the Casino in those days, some guests would walk to the hotel bar between dances and partake of ice-cream sodas and a variety of soft drinks, though after 1927 alcoholic drinks were served surreptitiously and illegally. A fancy dress or masquerade ball was held at the Casino every summer, usually in August. Some people went to endless trouble about their costumes while others, especially the young bachelors, behaved rather as one did on shipboard in the old days — creating a last-minute effect with blackened face and an old curtain.

High Diving at Katy's Cove. C.P.R.

There was no swimming pool at the *Algonquin*, of course, but there was Katy's Cove, perhaps colder then than it is today — there was not much algae — with plenty of mud on the bottom, and one or two rows of shabby bathhouses. Mr. Fred McCurdy was the boss of it all — a short, thin man wearing a white coat and carrying an armful of large bath towels with a huge "C.P.R." on them, which he handed out to the swimmers. Mrs. McCurdy worked there too, selling ice-cream cones and candy. Later, Mr. Jardine — no one used his first name, which was Jack — took over Katy's Cove, where he also taught swimming and lifesaving. For many years he came with his family for the summers, a man who insisted upon discipline from the young and from his own staff.

It was considered *the thing* to swim only in the morning, the fashionable time. The townspeople and their children were able to use Katy's Cove only in the afternoons, when the bathhouses were unlocked for them at two p.m. — a rule which makes me blush to recall.

One of the best things at Katy's Cove was the big raft. There was the first raft and then the far or big raft with its high and low diving boards and a chute covered with canvas tacked onto wood. We hauled up an old bucket filled with water, poured it down the chute to wet

A tea party at Fort Tipperary.
From left to right: Helen Thompson Balfour;
Bea Hanson Bond; the Hon. Marguerite
Shaughnessy; Alice Thompson Wilson;
[unknown]. Private Collection

it, and then slid down either sitting up, lying down, or even standing. But the bath houses really *were* shabby, even though they improved over the years. Young girls spent long times hanging bath towels or clothes over the knot holes to prevent their friends or boy cousins from peeking through. Shabby or not, however, some of the more important guests had bathhouses reserved for them.

The most exciting moment of a Katy's Cove morning was at eleven-fifty or perhaps twelve noon, when the C.P.R. daily train steamed across the causeway which separated the Cove from the open Bay. The engineer blew his whistle and everyone, children and adults, waved furiously. Another pleasure was that the hotel orchestra played at the beach in the mornings.

It was fun running down the old gravel path through the woods to the beach. This later became a boardwalk and was very slippery when wet. But there was always a race to see who could be there first in the mornings. On Sundays the service at Greenock Church was shorter and so the Presbyterians were ready and changed at Katy's Cove before the Anglicans or others. Swimming races were most important and taken very seriously — the favourite being the tub race in old cut-off beer barrels with wooden paddles. The contestants kept going round in circles.

The summer children sometimes played golf with their parents, while their friends among the town children earned pocket money as caddies. There were no golf carts in those days, neither the electric nor the pull kind. Many of those caddies turned into excellent golfers — as well as shrewd judges of human character as they followed the rich and famous around the course.

At the end of the season a prize-giving was held at the Casino for tennis, swimming, and sometimes golf competitions. This was a great occasion with some notable person presenting the prizes, and the boys and girls waiting, uncomfortable but also excited and self-important in their best clothes.

One year, two of the smaller summer children received particular attention and even notoriety. One was George Neuflize St. Lawrence Ponsonby, the youngest son — and born in Canada — of the Governor General Lord Bessborough and Lady Bessborough. Other children, of course, nicknamed him "No Fleas!" The Bessboroughs rented *Maplehurst*, the house later owned by the Gills, for the summer of 1934. The other child was the small son of the Hon. William Herridge, Canadian Minister to the U.S.A. in Washington, and his wife Mildred (the sister of Prime Minister R.B. Bennet). They had a house on Harriet Street, later owned by Mr. A.J. Kirk.

The tragedy of the Lindbergh kidnapping in 1932 was still much in the news and on people's minds, and both Lord Bessborough and Mr. Herridge had received threatening letters about their own sons. So, although both families decided to summer in St. Andrews, where there were no crowds, a detective was nevertheless assigned to each child. The Bessboroughs had a Mountie and the Herridges a Secret Service man in plain clothes, but both wore white panama hats!

What excitement there was among the children, the nurses, and nursemaids! The two young men were on every picnic, every walk, and of course at Katy's Cove. Each stood outside his small charge's bathhouse during dressing and undressing; the little boys were then carried down to the water and back again when it was time to leave. When the Bessboroughs' Mountie took a day off, a local St. Andrews Mountie took over. The large black English pram, with young George sleeping in it, was out on the lawn, while *our* Mountie, complete with scarlet jacket and uniform hat, sat beside him in a rocker. At least once he was observed to be reading a mystery magazine.

The summer cottage children were always in awe of "the hotel" and were rather nervous if asked to a meal there by young *Algonquin* guests. Some of the cottages had their mail directed to the hotel, and it was collected from the front desk, which saved a walk down to the post office. We felt very important if asked to go and fetch the mail. Occasionally, if we had a friend in the hotel, there would be races down the seemingly endless corridors; and best of all, Noni

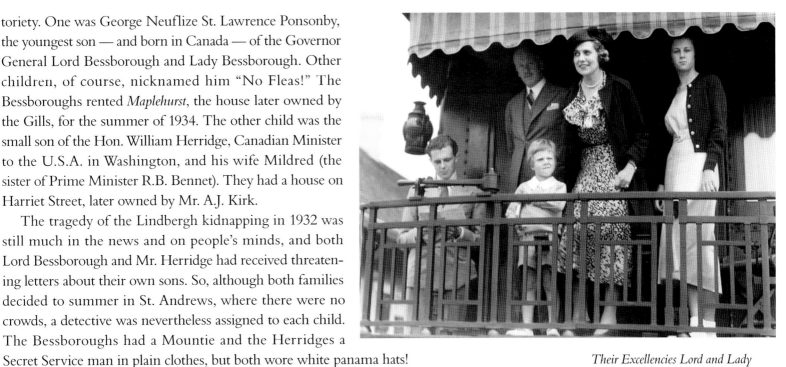

Their Excellencies Lord and Lady Bessborough; Viscount Duncannon (Eric); the Hon. Neuflize Ponsonby; Lady Moira Ponsonby. C.P.R.

Marion Forgan (right) and friend, early 1900s. Private Collection

Shean, the telephone operator for many years, might allow us to operate the hotel telephone in its tiny cubicle behind the front desk. I don't know what the hotel guests thought of this.

Going around to the back door of the *Algonquin*, we would usually find one of St. Andrews' most famous characters and one much beloved by children. This was Caddy Norris, who might be taking away the garbage or delivering ice to the hotel. He called at Katy's Cove each day for the same reasons. Caddy was a black man who had been born with a harelip and a cleft palate, making him difficult to understand sometimes. In those days when first names were not usual, Caddy broke the convention: the Hon. Marguerite Shaughnessy was always "Marg" to Caddy. He had a strong team of horses and the favourite thing to do was to ride on the back of Caddy's flat wagon. Even the strictest nanny seemed to think it all right if her charges rode part of the way up the hill with Caddy.

In the afternoons, the summer children usually went to play at the Block House, building sand castles and climbing and playing games in the "Big Hotel" — the clump of red sandstone rocks at Niger Reef. The reef seemed very large in those far-off days; perhaps it is smaller now, washed down by the tides. Near the Block House the fat black cannons were just meant for climbing on, and many an old photograph album has the family lined up astride them. Sadly, the originals were moved to the Town Hall and the replacements are ugly things.

Wading was considered tremendous fun. For beach wear children wore a sort of yellow romper with a bib, made out of oilskin like the old fishermen's hats, sticky and not very water-proof. The girls' dresses were shoved into the rompers. There were also a few bath houses not far from the Block House, on the water near the bottom of Adolphus Street. Made of wood and painted dark red, they were owned by Miss Elspa Friar, who rented them out. At high tide some people did bathe from these, but the water was very cold and not always clean.

The sun was considered dangerous, and straw hats were worn by the children. The white straw from last year would be shellacked black, or japanned, for this year, and consequently smelt of varnish in the sun.

Picnics were not casual affairs but were planned well ahead, and there were usually twenty or thirty people of all ages. There were no barbecues in those days. People did not sit on verandahs or terraces and have meals outside: no hot dogs or hamburgers. There was a large fire on which to toast marshmallows and perhaps cook a sausage on a stick in the coals. Heavy tartan steamer rugs were placed on the beach or the ground, while huge wicker picnic baskets with enamel plates and real cutlery were opened up. The favourite soft drink was ginger

beer in stone bottles and Sussex ginger ale with Welch's grape juice, half and half, always hard-boiled eggs and sandwiches, and marvellous homemade cakes and cookies. These were usually bought from Miss Susan Mowat and Miss Annie Campbell at *Elm Corner*. They came in sweater boxes from Miss O'Neill's store — great for serving them in. (Today sweaters are bought in plastic bags, which is very sad.) If we were lucky enough to be sent to *Elm Corner* to pick up the picnic cakes, we would linger, stroking the ladies' beautiful and famous cats. The all-grey ones were called "This," "That," and "Thuther," while the all-black ones were called "Pot" and "Kettle."

Most families did not have cars, so McQuoid's buckboard was usually hired for picnics. At one time it had been drawn by horses, but the McQuoid men had converted it to a motorized vehicle. We sat facing each other on long seats covered with rather soiled beige canvas. It was quite open to the sun, wind, or rain, though later on there was a roof with canvas curtains that could be rolled down. Two picnickers would sometimes sit up front with one of the McQuoid

Straw-hatted Magee and Robinson children with their nurse, Agnes, 1919. Private Collection

brothers, Henry, Hope, or Jim. But best of all were the back two steps, high off the ground, with two looped iron handles, one on each side. What bliss it was if Henry McQuoid would let one of us stand there and hang on tight! Mostly, alas, it was one of the boys.

Besides the McQuoid men, much afflicted by laughing, teasing, excited children, there were two private chauffeurs — the Norman Wilsons' Clifford, very long-suffering, and Tedley, a much more severe man, who drove for Mrs. Andrew Allan and her grandchildren. Both wore chauffeur's caps and a sort of beige dustcoat. There were others, too, but these are the best remembered.

Favourite picnic spots were O'Neill's Farm, Kilmarnock Head, Oven Head, Holt's Point, and New River Beach. Boat picnics were an even greater excitement. Capt. Finigan's boat was the best for hire, and on special occasions we went out on deep-sea fishing parties — huge cod being hauled up by tiny people with assistance from an adult, Capt. Finigan being everywhere at once, helping to bait the heavy hooks lowered to the bottom and then pulled up six feet. Prizes of twenty-five cents or ten cents or five cents were offered for the first, the biggest, the

"Cuthbert" or "Cuthy," the Rea boys' famous car.

most — and even the smallest. We would fill a large wooden bin with fish in a short time. Favourite landing places for picnics were Pendleton Beach, McMaster (otherwise known as Ayscough or Mac Island), and sometimes the far side of Navy Island.

Many hours were also spent fishing from the town wharf, where we caught flounders and sculpins. Since the latter might sting, there were lots of shouts for help.

Climbing Chamcook Mountain was another thing the young loved to do, carving their initials and the date on the smooth rocks at the very top. The earliest initials were dated 1784 and were surrounded by a heart and the initials "A.W.W." and "H.E.W." Nearly all the smooth rocks were inscribed. Were they brothers, sisters, friends, or lovers? Returning to the mountain, sometimes after many years, you looked nostalgically for your initials. So much simple pleasure shared by so many people. Alas, no more. The rocks were sandblasted by the former owners of the *Rossmount Hotel* and of the mountain. What a cruel and wanton thing to do!

Movies were held at the Andraleo Hall — with Prof. Russell playing the piano during the silent era — and later at the more modern Marina Theatre on Water Street. But children mostly made their own fun, such as the baseball games played most evenings on the lawn near the back door of the *Algonquin*. They even formed gangs, which fought furiously some summers and could be merciless to newcomers.

One trip per summer to St. Stephen and Calais was a special outing — sharing the cost of McQuoid's taxi. A visit to Jane Todd's in Calais for ice-cream soda was a must. When later we took trips in private cars, the driving could be erratic. In December 1922, the New Brunswick government changed driving on the roads from the left side to the right, that month being chosen because traffic was light and there would be less confusion. Until the change, the carriage horses crossing the International Bridge from St. Stephen would automatically switch to the right side halfway across and continue into Maine. Some of us have memories of brothers and cousins who learned to drive at sixteen and were not quite as adaptable as the horses.

The roads were not paved, of course, and sometimes the dust was terrible. In St. Andrews the unpaved streets were a raspberry red; after rain the red clay was soft and messy, so that the soles of our white socks were stained all summer long — it would not wash out.

Those summers in St. Andrews between the Wars were feats of organization and planning. Behind the excited children who counted each day to the holiday, wondering who was going to be there *this* year, parents and their staffs made mighty preparations. High trunks, low steamer trunks, wardrobe trunks (with clothes hanging on one side and three small drawers

Train waiting at St. Andrews Station, c. 1920. Charlotte County Archives

and one large one on the other), hat boxes with round mesh forms on either side — all these would be brought down from attics or up from basements, weeks before departure. Bed linen, blankets, towels, flat silver, and favourite cooking utensils would be packed for those renting cottages. Summer dresses were usually made by a seamstress who came to the house for several days. In the days before drip-dry clothing and no-iron sheets, a lot of everything was needed.

Most families left the cities during the last week in June. Those from Montreal always tried to avoid leaving on June 24th, St. Jean Baptiste Day, because of the parades and crowds. Windsor Station would be full of travellers, and it was not unusual to find at least four private cars en route to St. Andrews on the same night — *Saskatchewan*, the Van Hornes' car; *Killarney*, the Shaughnessys' car; *Mount Royal*, Miss Olive Hosmer's company car; and Senator Cairine Wilson's government car with Mr. Norman Wilson, eight children, and staff.

Breakfast in the dining car was a special excitement — white tablecloths, shining cutlery, water carafes with flip-up tops, coffee cups and milk glasses jiggling with the motion of the train. It was always a big moment when the trainman walked through the dining car, removed his uniform cap, and held it across his chest in a manner similar to the President of the United States taking a salute. Then there was the scary walk along the train, the cars swinging to and fro, the jump over the metal part dividing the cars. The dining car seemed so far away. Yet somehow we arrived, scared but triumphant.

Few children today can know the exquisite thrill of an overnight train journey — those kind and wonderful black porters, the complicated letting-down of upper berths, making them up with sheets and blankets, hanging the heavy green curtains, moving the ladder along for passengers to climb in and out of those upper berths; the communal washrooms, the fascination of watching strangers cleaning their teeth, washing necks and arms, putting false teeth in and out — such sights were extraordinary to the young.

The dining car went off at Mattawamkeag. Then came Vanceboro, with immigration officials, followed by the most dramatic moment on the way to St. Andrews — the arrival at McAdam Junction. Here was a very large, turreted Victorian stone station. The porters put down the steps for the Pullman cars, took dusters and wiped the handrails on either side, and cheerful as all get out handed down the passengers to the platform. You could smell the different air. It was fresh. It was New Brunswick, of course!

We wanted to rush right off to the circular stone pond and see if the large and ancient turtle was still there. But those of us with parents who had themselves travelled to St. Andrews as children would immediately be paraded before Miss Flora Grant, a short stout lady, and a Scotswoman of some stature. Miss Grant ran the *McAdam Station Hotel* and restaurant. It was said at that time that no C.P.R. official, from the president down, would have failed to pay his respects at McAdam to Miss Grant. Urged to be polite and to speak up and give our names, we shook hands with her.

Behind, in the station dining room, were an amazing number of tables with their white tablecloths set and ready. Who on earth could be eating all those breakfasts? *We* had already

Bar Road Station, c. 1925.
Young people accompanied their departing sweethearts to this stop before disembarking and trudging the lonely two miles back to St. Andrews. Notman Photo, McCord Museum

eaten on our train. But suddenly the doors would be flung open and a great rush of people entered — of course, the Boston train had arrived. They only had a short time to gobble down their breakfasts and come along with us to St. Andrews (or catch a train for Saint John). Meanwhile, the St. Andrews cars had been uncoupled from the Montreal-Saint John train and put on another track — all very confusing to a child.

McAdam seemed so very big, and the platforms swirled with the steam from several trains. If you looked at the turtle too long there was perhaps a moment of panic that you might not get on the right train, might not find your family. Was this perhaps good training for the future, for the vast airport crowds at Toronto, Boston, Atlanta, Heathrow?

The St. Andrews train stopped at all the small wayside stations — Lawrence Station, Watt Junction, Rollingdam, and Elmsville. Most children of that era seem to remember Watt Junction best, probably because the train had another long stop there while the St. Stephen section was uncoupled. Each year the same two cats seemed to be sitting on the same door-step. Exactly the same two hens pecked and clucked at the same farmhouse door. Fields of daisies and buttercups grew right up to the tracks. These sights were so important to us. And at last we would be creeping like a long snake around Chamcook Lake. In some cases you could almost reach out and put your hand in the window of one of the small houses or camps clustered along the tracks. At the Bar Road we made another stop, where a roofed shelter and long wooden bench were painted in barn red, the C.P.R. colour, and here the Van Horne, Maxwell, and Hope families, if they were on board, would disembark. Then off again — and as the whistle blew, the people at Katy's Cove waved and shouted.

At last we had reached St. Andrews! Taxis were drawn up to meet us. Along to the baggage car to collect a beloved dog or cat — though one little girl rented a kitten for the summer and returned it when she went home. The heavy trunks and bicycles would follow us in McQuoid's truck. How *did* Henry McQuoid and his men ever manage? On to the hotels, the summer cottages, the rented ones. The lilac season was almost over. the Block House was still there. The Greenock Church steeple and the tall water tower of the *Algonquin* still stood above the town. Another summer had begun!

Opposite: A view of St. Andrews from the northwest, c. 1900. St. Andrews Biological Station

First Owners of Houses as indicated on map

1. Thompson, F.W.★
2. Inness, George Jr. ★
3. Shaughnessy, Lord★
4. Hosmer, C.R.★
5. Smith, C.F.★
6. Markey, F.H.★
7. McMaster, Donald★
8. Wheelock, T.R.★
9. Heney, Theodore
10. Cowan, Charles
11. Smith, Jeremiah★
12. Smoot, L.E.★
13. Dodd, R.
14. Seely, D.B.
15. Southam, H.S.
16. Gardiner, R.S.★
17. Forgan, D.R.★
18. Cobb, E.H.
19. Reed, Hayter★
20. Reed, Gordon★
21. Tilley, Sir Leonard★
22. Everett, C.S.★
23. MacLaren, the Misses
24. Shuter, George
25. Smith, E. Atherton
26. Thorp, Harry
27. Reed, Gordon★
28. Sills, Dean Charles Morton
29. Walker, Mrs. Edward C.
30. Macklem, O.R.
31. Guthrie, Norman G.★

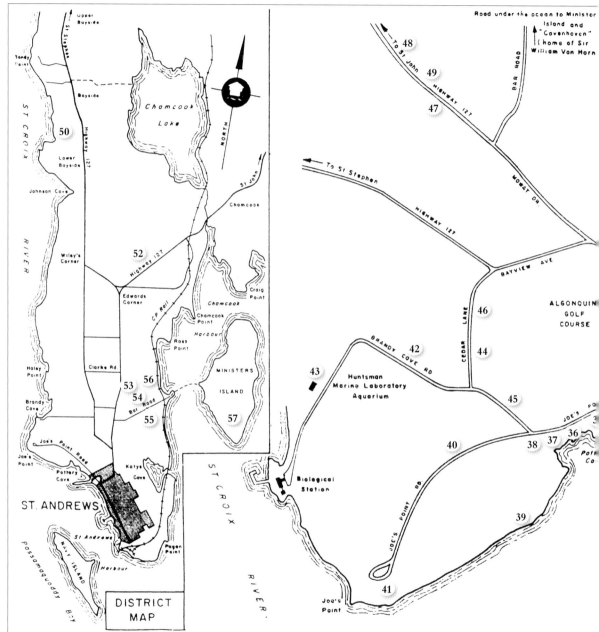

DISTRICT MAP

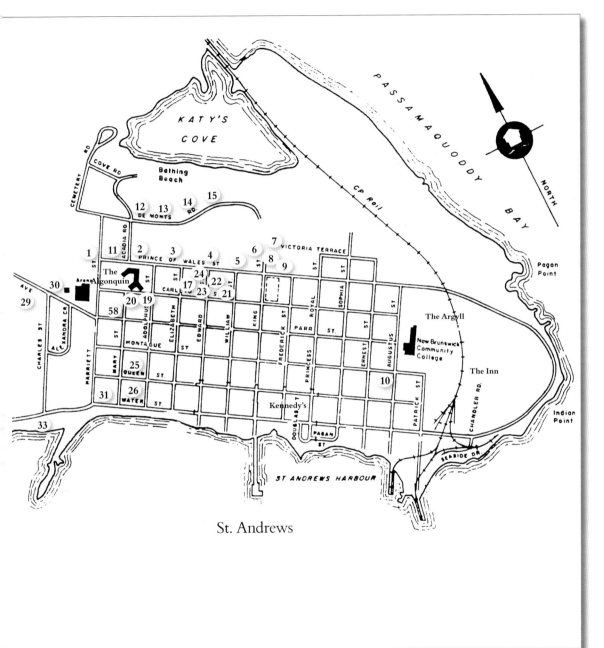

St. Andrews

32. Topp, William H.
33. Marshall, Thomas
34. Childs, Mrs. Sarah
35. Russell, G. Horne★
36. Freeman, Halstead
37. Magee, Col. Allan A.
38. Breese, William L.
39. Eidlitz, Ernest
40. Wainwright, Mrs. Arnold
41. Christie, Miss Katherine
42. Tait, Sir Thomas★
43. Hume, Col. Frank★
44. Bowser, the Rev. Alexander T.★
45. Gordon, Blair
46. Huntsman, Dr. A.G.★
47. Hoar, Prof. Emery★
48. Tupper, Sir Charles★
49. Mackay, Senator Robert★ and Wilson, Miss Cairine★
50. Ross, Frank M.★
51. Shaughnessy, the Hon. Ann★
52. Ross, the Rev. H.P.★
53. Leighton, Delmar★
54. Hope, William★
55. Hope, Charles
56. Maxwell, Edward★
57. Van Horne, Sir William★
58. Knight, Miss Sarah Maria★

★ Chapters on these families and their summer homes are included in this book. Information on the remaining houses can be found in the Appendix.

Sarah M. Knight and Thomasina R. Andrews

This most unpretentious house was built in 1825 and has given shelter and happiness to several families, influencing their lives in its quiet way.

The Rev. John Cummings was the first parish priest in St. Andrews (1825-1836) and this house was the Roman Catholic rectory. It belonged to the Church until 1880. Some time during that period, the ornate ceiling in one of the downstairs rooms was decorated in various colours in the Italian style. This room was probably used as a small chapel.

The Rectory was sold in 1880 to Sarah Maria Knight and remained in the Knight family until 1897. The interesting family group on the steps of the house in the accompanying picture of the *Anchorage* shows Miss Marjorie Knight, later of New River Beach, New Brunswick, who is the babe-in-arms. The photograph was taken about 1889. Miss Knight, a well-known and much-admired New Brunswicker, identified almost all the people in the group when in her late nineties — a formidable feat of memory.

In 1897 the Knights sold the house to Mrs. Thomasina R. Andrews, wife of Capt. Frederick G. Andrews (Mariner). The Andrews named it the *Anchorage* and the small house next door the *Haven,* two fitting names for a seafaring family. Thomasina Andrews was a remarkable woman. Believed to be one of the first women to receive her navigational papers, she frequently went to sea as a young wife with her husband and later became an outstanding citizen of St. Andrews.

Since there were not many cottages for rent in those days in St. Andrews, Mrs. Andrews wisely decided to let the *Anchorage* each summer, while she and her sister, Miss Main, moved into the *Haven.* Mrs. Andrews did this every year until the house was sold to Mrs. Alice Payne in 1929. Mrs. Robert Gill, of Ottawa, rented it around 1908, and her young sons loved it, as all children did. Evan Gill, one of those sons, returned many years later on his retirement from the Department of External Affairs and became a permanent resident of St. Andrews. Mrs. George F. Smith and her family, from Saint John, rented the *Anchorage* every summer from 1914 to 1925.

Opposite: The Haddock and Knight families on the steps of the Anchorage, 1889. Miss Marjorie Knight is the babe-in-arms.

Private Collection

In 1936 Robert (Bob) Gardiner Payne and his wife, née Alice Winthrop, owned the *Anchorage*, and Alice modernized and furnished the house attractively. At this time the front steps were moved to the side and a cedar hedge planted to fill the space.

Bob Payne was born in Japan, where his father, William T. Payne, lived and worked for forty-three years. (He represented the Canadian Pacific Steamship Company in both China and Japan.) Bob Payne was also the grandson of Robert Sylvester Gardiner, who built the first summer cottage in St. Andrews in 1893. During the Second World War, when Bob Payne served in the U.S. Navy at the Headquarters of Eastern Seaboard Command — he had been a naval aviator during the First World War — the Paynes were of course unable to travel to St. Andrews. But after 1945, Bob came every summer, insisting upon driving his own car from New Jersey until his 88th year. He was one of St. Andrews' oldest and longest-standing summer visitors when he died on January 15, 1988, at the age of ninety.

Mrs. Hope Dawson, Bob Payne's sister, spent a couple of years in the *Anchorage* during the Second World War with her three children — Robert, Margaret (Meg), and Elizabeth (Betty) all of whom remembered St. Andrews with affection. Their father, David Livingston Dawson, was with the Chartered Bank of India, Australia & China in Hong Kong. After the Japanese captured the city, he spent the rest of the war in an internment camp.

Betty Dawson married Gordon Maxwell from an old New Brunswick family. They bought a small house in the 1950s and lived in St. Andrews for several years.

Two other families with strong St. Andrews connections rented the *Anchorage* jointly for part of the Second World War: the Ballantynes and the Gordons. The Ballantynes bought the Bowser house in 1944 and became permanent residents of St. Andrews. Meanwhile, Blair and Mary Gordon bought land from the Bowser estate just down the hill from the Ballantynes, where they built their house in 1945.

Blair Gordon, who became president of Dominion Textiles, was the son of Sir Charles and Lady Gordon of Montreal. Sir Charles had formerly been president of the Bank of Montreal. Blair and Mary were both good golfers, especially Mary. She competed in most of the St. Andrews tournaments, in the New Brunswick Provincial Ladies events, and at Mt. Bruno in Montreal. She also greatly enjoyed their summer house, *Elbow Bend*, and was a fine gardener, a flower arranger of almost professional quality, and a first-class bridge player.

In July 1987, the *Anchorage* was sold to Mr. and Mrs. Robert Stevens from Pennsylvania, continuing the fine tradition of this treasured old house.

Mrs. George F. Smith and the Magee and Robinson Families

Mrs. George F. Smith of Saint John was one of the early guests at the *Algonquin Hotel*. She brought her three young daughters to stay there in July 1892 — Constance Gordon Smith, twelve; Amy Gordon Smith, ten; and Madeleine Leslie (Bebe) Smith, eight. This was the first of many such visits when they were children.

Mrs. Smith's husband, George Frederick Smith, died in 1894 at age fifty-five, leaving his widow of forty-five to bring up their daughters alone. George F. Smith's Loyalist grandfather, Dr. Nathan Smith, who practised as a physician in Rhode Island and Massachusetts, had espoused the King's cause at the outbreak of the Revolutionary War and served throughout as a Surgeon Major in the 1st Battalion of DeLancey's Brigade. After the war ended in 1781, Dr. Smith joined other officers and men of the disbanded Loyalist unit on half pay and in 1783 settled in what is now the city of Saint John. There he practised as a physician and also maintained an apothecary's shop at Lower Cove.

Nathan Smith's only son, by a second marriage, was Thomas M. Smith, who became a partner in the firm of Johnson & Walker, ship chandlers and ship owners. When he died, his own son, George F. Smith, took over the business and expanded it. As a prominent ship owner in Saint John, he was one of the first to own and operate iron and steel-clad steam vessels, of which the *Timandra* (1885) and the *Andromeda* (1889) were especially well known. A tall, good-looking man, he became an alderman of the City of Saint John. He was also a fine athlete and an active member of the famous Neptune Rowing Club, the Saint John Athletic club, and the Bonaventure Salmon Club on the Bonaventure River in the Gaspé — where he fished avidly for salmon, in what became known as Smith's Pool.

While fishing on the Bonaventure on June 20, 1877, he received the following telegram from Saint John: "Send for Smith immediately. Half the City, including his stores are destroyed by fire. House probably safe. Signed Thos. Adams."

This telegram was sent by the Montreal Telegraph Company in Saint John to Cascapedia,

Mrs. George F. Smith
in the Anchorage garden with
three daughters, 1918.
Left to right: Constance (Mrs. G.D.
Robinson); Bebe (Mrs. A.A. Magee);
Amy (Mrs. N.G. Guthrie). Private Collection

which was probably the nearest telegraph office to the Bonaventure Salmon Club. Two Indian runners were hired to carry the message. R. H. Montgomery, who was at the telegraph office in Cascapedia, sent a note with the runners that read: "This is bad news. I deeply sympathize with you. I fear your loss will be a heavy one."

George F. Smith married Wilhelmina Gordon of Pictou, Nova Scotia, in October 1879. Wilhelmina Gordon's grandparents had come from Scotland to Pictou in 1816, at the time of the Clearances. They had lived at Kildonan in Sutherland. Wilhelmina had two sisters and three brothers; one brother, Daniel M. Gordon, became an eminent Presbyterian minister who was appointed Principal of Queen's University in Kingston in 1903.

On the death of George F. Smith, his wife and daughters continued to live at 110 Union Street in Saint John. Constance married Guy D. Robinson of Saint John, and later they moved to Montreal. Amy married Norman G. Guthrie of Guelph, Ontario, and they lived in Ottawa. Bebe married Allan Angus Magee from London, Ontario, and they lived in Montreal. Guy Robinson was a grain broker while Norman Guthrie and Allan Magee were lawyers.

All three Smith daughters encouraged their husbands to summer in St. Andrews, and two of them later built houses there. From 1914 to 1925, however, Wilhelmina Gordon Smith rented the *Anchorage* and shared it with two of her daughters and her grandchildren.

The house was not really large but had a lot of small rooms. The Robinson family were on one side of the staircase and the Magees on the other. Grannie Smith had the large room on the ground floor to the left of the front door, the one with the colourful ceiling. The Guthries did not stay at the *Anchorage*, as they had their own house on Water Street.

There were, however, seven children under the age of twelve in the house at one time and four Guthries who visited. Looking back, the children remembered the goodness and kindness of their grandmother; every summer seemed to be better than the last one.

But there were sad years too — especially for the Magee family. The First World War separated Bebe and Allan Magee for three years. He had gone overseas in 1916 in command of the 148th Battalion from Montreal; although the battalion did not go to France as a unit, Col. Magee saw service at the front in all the major battles and was on the staff of Gen. Sir Arthur Currie, Commander-in-Chief of the Canadian Forces.

The Magee children — James, Willa, and Nora — were all born between 1912 and 1915 and did not see their father until his return in 1919.

It was particularly comforting for Bebe Magee to come to St. Andrews during those summers and to be with her mother and sisters. In 1920 she gave birth to their second son, Allan Gordon Magee — the small child sitting at the foot of the *Anchorage* steps in the accompanying photograph — who gave much happiness to his family. Two years later, however, they suffered the grievous loss of their eldest boy, James, at the age of ten. He had suffered courageously through several periods of severe illness, and his personality had made a great impact upon many people.

Grannie Smith died in 1925 at the *Anchorage*. She had the love and care of her three daughters during her last days. They remembered her exceptional qualities: how she had inherited from her Gordon ancestors intelligence, dignity, charm of manner, and a keen sense of humour; how as a young widow she had proved her strength and sound business sense while handling all the family's affairs; how she became an excellent public speaker with a most gracious way of presiding over committees and public meetings. They remembered her straight back and beautiful carriage — and those strict instructions to her grandchildren to "sit up and don't slouch!" The grandchildren, ranging from age sixteen down, were all heartbroken when she died. Their grandmother had been such a safe and loving part of their lives.

During the next eight years the Allan Magee family continued to come to St. Andrews, but they rented a different house each time. After Norman Guthrie's death in 1929, it was *Croix Crest*, the Guthrie house. But in 1943 they were finally able to build their own house on Joe's Point Road near Pottery Creek, which they named the *Little House*. Over the years they would add to it three times.

Col. Allan A. Magee, C.B.E., D.S.O., Q.C., was an eminent Montreal lawyer and a director of many companies. After his distinguished service in the First World War, he was Executive Assistant to the Minister of National Defence, the Hon. J.L. Ralston, during the Second World War. Madeleine Leslie (Bebe) Magee was equally well known in Montreal — as the chairman of many organizations and a hard worker for the Canadian Red Cross in both World Wars. In their own house — and with ten grandchildren — their summers in St. Andrews had extra meaning for them, when their greatest pleasure was to sit on the terrace and watch the unending tides come and go. Allan Magee died on June 3, 1961, and Bebe Magee just eighteen months later on December 5, 1962.

The first of the Magee offspring to build in St. Andrews was Nora Elizabeth. She married William Lawrence Breese from Washington, D.C., on October 19, 1939, in Montreal. He served with the U.S.A.A.F. during the Second World War. They built their summer cottage

Allan G. Magee, aged two, sitting on the steps of the Anchorage, 1922. Private Collection

in 1942 on Joe's Point Road, next door to where the Allan Magee cottage was to be situated, and called it *Pottery Creek*. In this beloved cottage their children — Belinda, Peter, and Penelope — spent all their childhood summers.

Later, Bill and Nora Breese bought another house for the family on Bayside at Wiley's Corner. To this house the family continued to come with their children — from as far away as London, Washington, and Africa — into the fifth generation.

Pottery Creek was sold, and Bill and Nora Breese moved to Harding's Point, where they had bought the Eidlitz house, in 1971. Two years earlier, Nora bought the old bakery building on Water Street and with her sister, Willa, opened a boutique, which they called *La Baleine* and ran together for ten years. Nora Breese died in Washington on January 17, 1980, at age sixty-five.

Willa Magee married David H. Walker on July 27, 1939, in Montreal. Capt. Walker, from Scotland, was in the Black Watch. During the Second World War, he was a prisoner of war in Germany for five years, making several escapes and planning others — for which he was awarded the M.B.E. Willa Walker was Senior Staff Officer of the R.C.A.F. Women's Division, serving from 1941 to 1944, and was also awarded the M.B.E. After the war the Walkers went to India with their eldest son, Giles, and Maj. Walker became Comptroller first to the Viceroy, Lord Wavell, and then briefly to Lord Mountbatten (the last Viceroy). When David Walker retired as a regular officer in 1947, he decided to start a new career as a writer, and the family returned to Canada. They moved to St. Andrews in June 1948, accompanied by their two Scottish-born sons, Giles and seven-month-old Barclay.

David Walker achieved great success as a writer; he published more than twenty novels and many short stories, while several films have been made from his work. He was twice awarded the Governor General's Award for Fiction. Indeed, by 1955 the books had permitted the Walkers to buy a beautiful piece of land just outside St. Andrews and build their own house, which they named *Strathcroix*. In July 1987, David Walker was made a Member of the Order of Canada. He died in 1992 after a lengthy battle with emphysema.

Two more sons were born in Charlotte County — David in 1949 and Julian in 1951 — and all four boys attended the local primary school in St. Andrews and were brought up there. Two became permanent residents. David and Willa Walker's ten grandchildren live in the town or visit frequently — another fifth generation family.

Allan Gordon Magee was the third member of the Magee family to return to St. Andrews. During the Second World War, he joined the Royal Canadian Regiment at the age of nineteen and was posted overseas at age twenty, fighting all through the campaigns in Sicily and the Italian mainland and becoming the youngest Brigade Major in the Canadian army. He also served in northwest Europe, after which he was awarded the M.B.E.

In 1944 Allan Magee married Phoebe Anne Freeman from Montreal. She had joined the R.C.A.F. Women's Division in 1942 and was serving in Britain with the Canadian Bomber Group — so they were married at the Bomber station. Postwar for Allan meant first Bishop's University, then working in the brewing and distilling business. He and his wife had three children: Willa and twins Margot and Brian. Brian was killed in a helicopter crash at the age of twenty-five.

In 1969 Allan and Phoebe Magee came to St. Andrews to live and work. They bought the Misses Rigby's large and historic house on Queen Street; the following year, Allan bought the well-known gift shop, the *Sea Captain's Loft*, on Water Street, which he ran successfully until it was sold in 1983. As their home was too large for two people, they built a new and charming house next door. But Allan was to enjoy it for only seven weeks before his death on December 2, 1987.

The two grandchildren of Allan and Phoebe Magee have also spent much time in St. Andrews — making this another fifth generation family.

Mr. and Mrs. Guy Robinson, who had also shared the *Anchorage*, decided in 1922 to rent *Invernenty*, a delightful small house right on the waterfront which belonged to Mrs. T.J. Coughey. They would continue to rent it for eighteen years.

Guy de Lancey Robinson was a well-known grain broker in Montreal, his firm being Robinson & Climo. He and his wife, Constance, had three children — F. Barclay, Margaret (Peggy) de Lancey, and Helen Gordon — born between 1912 and 1920. After the Second World War and after their children had grown up, Guy and Constance Robinson continued to come to St. Andrews. Guy Robinson came alone after the death of his wife in 1955, a familiar guest at the *Algonquin* until his death in Montreal in 1960.

One of the Robinson children returned to build a house in St. Andrews – Margaret (Peggy), who on June 30, 1937, married Theodore Roosevelt Meighen, son of Senator Arthur Meighen, the former Prime Minister. The Meighens bought the Allan A. Magee property on Joe's Point Road from Allan Gordon Magee, moved the *Little House* there, and built a new all-season house on the site. It was finished by June 30, 1967, their thirtieth wedding anniversary. Each summer Michael Arthur Meighen, their son, and his wife, Kelly, brought their sons, Theodore (Teddy), Hugh, and Max, to occupy the former Magee house (once more enlarged) — making yet another fifth generation family.

Through Teddy Roosevelt Meighen's generosity, the Themadel Foundation (later, the T.R. Meighen Foundation) is based in St. Andrews. Due to wise administration, it has unobtrusively done a great deal of good in the community and further afield. Wonderfully supported by Peggy, Teddy will always be remembered as the quiet giver, diffident about every open-handed act he made possible. Teddy died in St. Andrews in 1979, and Peggy continued the family tradition of generosity. She later married Senator Hartland Molson, of Montreal; on her death in 2000, a warm memorial service was held in St. Andrews.

F. Barclay Robinson became a grain broker in his father's firm in Montreal, later working with container ships for C.A.S.T. During the Second World War, he was in the Royal Canadian Navy and stationed at Halifax. His wife, the former Ruth Seely, knew St. Andrews well. Her parents, Mr. and Mrs. D.B. Seely, had built a summer house on De Monts Road in 1912. Her grandfather was George Bosworth, vice-president of C.P.R. Steamships. Like a few other C.P.R. families, the Seelys used to travel to St. Andrews in a private railway car.

Barclay and Ruth Robinson had three sons — Gordon, Ian, and David (who died in 1956 at age twelve) — and six grandchildren. After Barclay's retirement, they moved to Lunenburg, Nova Scotia, where he died on July 31, 1988, at age seventy-six.

The St. Andrews connection has been maintained, however. Helen Gordon Robinson married John Kennet Starnes in 1941. They had two sons and have two grandchildren. John Starnes joined the Black Watch during the Second World War and served with Military Intelligence. After the war he joined External Affairs, being later appointed Canadian ambassador to Germany and to Egypt. In 1970 he became Director-General of the Security Service of the R.C.M.P. in Ottawa. On his retirement he took up writing and published several works of fiction. He and Helen visited St. Andrews frequently.

Lewis Egerton Smoot

12

Dayspring, 1929
De Monts Road

Mr. and Mrs. L.E. Smoot built *Dayspring*, their large house on the De Monts Road, in 1929. It had a low stone wall, and the garden with its paved walks was visible to all who passed by.

Lewis Egerton Smoot was president of the Sand & Gravel Corp., and he and his wife had their residence in Washington, D.C. Once *Dayspring* was completed, he rarely came to St. Andrews. Mrs. Smoot was a large lady who always wore a big hat, rather old-fashioned dresses, and small button boots. These boots were cleaned every day, and she was most particular about the soles: they had to be polished too. Each summer she had her granddaughters, Polly and Peggy MacNeale, as her guests. Good-looking, dark-haired girls, they came for the whole summer without their parents, and for the first few years did not mix much with other young people. They too dressed rather distinctively — in red sweaters, red tartan skirts, and black stockings.

When the Bermuda Squadron of the British Navy came to St. Andrews with H.M.S. *Norfolk*, Comm. Charles Brown and another officer from the ship were playing tennis at the *Algonquin* when they casually asked the MacNeale girls where they could swim. Polly and Peggy took them down to Katy's Cove. On the way home they suggested the officers come to tea with their grandmother — who was very hospitable and enjoyed guests.

A few days later the summer colony was electrified by the news that the handsome Comm. Brown had fallen in love at first sight with Polly MacNeale, aged sixteen, and she with him.

Mrs. Smoot was delighted. The girls' parents were summoned from Baltimore and set out immediately to meet Charles Brown. All was quickly arranged. Polly would attend school for one more year, then the Commander would retire from the Navy and they would be married. And that is what happened.

Sir James Hamet Dunn

12
Dayspring, 1929
De Monts Road

Sir James and Lady Dunn came to live in St. Andrews in 1947, after buying *Dayspring*, the former L.E. Smoot house.

James Hamet Dunn was born in Bathurst, New Brunswick, on October 29, 1874, and twenty-four years later he graduated with an LL.B. from Dalhousie Law School. But it had not been easy going. His family was not well off, and to make extra money Jimmy Dunn drove a carriage for Dr. Gideon Duncan in Bathurst — the old man took a special interest in the youth — and he even assisted at operations (occasionally administering chloroform). Much later, after he had become a rich industrialist, Sir James liked to reminisce about the exploits of the young Jimmy. A good-looking boy with vivid blue eyes, he was a friend of the young Max Aitken — later Lord Beaverbrook — and these two New Brunswickers hatched many plots and plans together, so that their careers were closely connected in the early days. Both responded to the lure of the stock exchange, and though James Dunn was admired as a skilful young lawyer, the financial markets soon won his main interest. It has been said of James Dunn that he began as a young man in a hurry, too impatient and too ambitious, though his character broadened with the years and was strengthened as he won prosperity and fame.

The first phase of his business career was described by his widow, Marcia Dunn, in her *Ballad of a Bathurst Boy*, written in 1956:

> In search of "gain" he went out West
> But roads back East fulfilled his quest —
> New York — the Mecca of the Dollar,
> With cane, cigar and velvet collar.
>
> Patent pearly buttoned boots,
> Posies gay in buttonholes —

Opposite: Dayspring from the air.
Wilson Studio, Saint John

65

Sir James Dunn. Private Collection

Curled and tilted jaunty brims,
Braided suits to suit your whims.

Break the strain of money making,
Take the reins and dare some racing —
In a neat affair for two,
Whirl along the Avenue.

This zest for living remained with him all his life.

In 1901 he married Gertrude Price, one of the four daughters of Herbert Molesworth Price, a member of the wealthy Price lumber family in Quebec. After living in Montreal, where James practiced law, the Dunns moved to England in 1905; two years later James founded the banking firm of Dunn, Fisher & Co. of London.

He was made a baronet in 1921. This was in recognition of the valuable work he had undertaken during the First World War — especially his fabled exploits in Scandinavia, where he saved for the Allies the Norwegian nickel the Germans so desperately needed.

Sir James Dunn adored his eldest daughter, Mona, whose striking portrait was painted by Sir William Orpen when she was twenty-three. In 1925 she married Edmund Tattersall, and they had one daughter, Monica. When Mona Tattersall died in 1928, her father was shattered. Indeed, his private life was deeply agitated during the 1920s, for his marriage to Gertrude Price was dissolved in December of 1925, and in the following year he married Irene Clarice, ex-Marchioness of Queensbury, in Paris.

They had one daughter, Anne, who inherited her father's love of New Brunswick, coming twice a year from New York, London, or Paris, to Nigadoo Lake near Bathurst. Her paintings have been shown at exhibitions in Fredericton, New York, and London. A charming person, gentle in manner, she has the same blue eyes as her father, to whom she shows a strong resemblance. She married twice: to Francis Wishart and to the artist Rodrigo Moynihan, with children by both marriages.

In Canada, the name of Sir James Dunn has mostly been associated with the Algoma Steel Corporation. In the 1930s there were lean and hard years, but Sir James had the vision to build Algoma up to greatness. The surprising thing is that he was not then a young man. Algoma was the labour of his sixties and seventies. These could have been the years to slow down, but for him this was the time of triumph and culmination. He saw his Algoma kingdom turn into an empire, and as president of the company made himself into a multi-millionaire.

After divorcing his second wife, James Dunn married Marcia Christoforides — or Christofor as she was affectionately called — on June 7, 1942. The new Lady Dunn had been a member of Sir James' staff since 1930; of Greek descent, she had classical beauty and was also very able. Her financial astuteness and keen appreciation of value rivalled the judgement of her husband. In informed circles it was acknowledged that she possessed one of the best financial brains in the country.

When the Dunns decided to buy *Dayspring* in 1947 and to make St. Andrews their home, Sir James was seventy-three years old and his wife thirty-seven. It was time to enjoy their life together, and St. Andrews was a good choice. They already had friends there; it was in Sir James' native New Brunswick and not too far from Bathurst, where he had a camp and ten thousand beloved acres. But by this time he had also become greatly concerned about privacy — and *Dayspring* was very exposed, right beside the De Monts Road on the way to Katy's Cove. So a nine-foot grey wooden fence was erected around the whole property, with one small gate at the side, which was always locked. The big entrance gates were also closed and locked. Friends invited to visit were told the exact time to arrive, and Lloyd Dougherty would be there to open the gates so that the cars could drive in. Meanwhile, a cedar hedge was planted — long since full-grown — on the inside of the fence.

Sir James had many a fetish about food. Parsley was a great thing at one time, and one greenhouse was devoted to parsley alone. He was convinced that it would make him live to be a hundred. When voyaging at sea, Sir James also insisted on drinking one cup of seawater daily and accompanied the sailor to the bow of the ship while a bucket was lowered and drawn — to make sure of what he was drinking.

Always fastidious about his clothes, he was proud of his small feet and specially made shoes.

Sir James exercised every day, and his endurance and energy were legendary. He could discuss some business deal long after midnight, then go out walking the next morning before his companions were awake. In St. Andrews, he walked down to Cockburn's Drug Store almost every morning at seven a.m. Bobby Cockburn would be sweeping the floor and getting ready for the day, and Sir James would read the morning newspaper in the back room. When he finished, he would telephone *Dayspring* and Lady Dunn would come to fetch him.

They made their shopping expeditions into town in a grey Rolls Royce; Lady Dunn at the wheel, wearing beautifully-cut jodhpurs and a pure silk shirt; Olymbia Kedros, Lady Dunn's sister, sitting in the back with Casanova, the white poodle; and Alexander, a rather unattractive and cross small brown pinscher, sitting with Sir James in the front. Mel Dougherty, who had his own butcher's shop at that time, would come out and take the meat order at the car window. Later on, when the Dunns had seven or more chihuahuas, a special roast would be ordered for the puppies' birthdays. Birthday candles would be stuck in the cooked meat and a party held around the kitchen table at *Dayspring*.

The Algoma company plane was stationed at Pennfield, just thirty minutes away from St. Andrews, and when a private cinema was installed at *Dayspring*, the plane would be dispatched to New York to pick up the latest and best film. Cinema night was a great treat for all the Dunns' friends, who sometimes saw films in St. Andrews before they reached Washington or Montreal.

There were also large cocktail parties at *Dayspring* in the summers. Guests could wan-

Cockburn's Store, on Water Street, c. 1876.
D. Will McKay

der out onto the terrace, and on the lawn guests were sometimes invited to throw wooden hoops over champagne bottles. In 1953, they were Möet & Chandon vintage 1943 Special Coronation Cuvée, with the royal crest and Elizabeth II Regina on the bottle. Sir James and Lady Dunn enjoyed visiting their friends and attending dinners and cocktail parties.

Both their portraits were painted by Salvador Dali. The painting of Christofor Dunn, mounted on a horse with a falcon strapped to her wrist, was called *Equestrian Fantasy* (1954); the portrait of her husband — called *La Turbie* (1949) — is rather startling, with Sir James posed in a bright yellow toga and his bare foot resting on a gold brick. He was rather shy about this picture and had it hung upstairs in the library. Only a few friends were allowed to see it.

These portraits, and another magnificent Dali called *Santiago El Grande*, are now in the Beaverbrook Art Gallery in Fredericton — only part of a collection donated by the Dunn Foundation.

It was a Dali painting which required Christofor Dunn — who could mastermind almost any operation — to be especially ingenious on one occasion. Some time in the early 1950s, Sir James had gone to the Soo (Sault Ste. Marie) for a few days and his wife wanted to surprise him with a new Dali. The painting in its frame was very large. It was also in New York and had to be transported to St. Andrews with all speed. A large container truck was therefore dispatched from Black's Harbour to collect and bring back the prize to *Dayspring*. Meanwhile, Stan Nickerson, a local contractor who had done a great deal of work at the house, was directed to open up the whole end wall of the library upstairs. It was to be hinged, so that after the painting was inside the wall could be quickly closed again. To prevent cold from penetrating the house — it must have been late autumn — a plastic sheet divided the library. Lady Dunn and Mrs. Kedros stayed on the warm side of the division while encouraging Nickerson's crew with hot drinks and doughnuts.

The job was all done in forty-eight hours, ready for Sir James's return. Lady Dunn had a long stool made specially for in front of the painting, with a beautiful gros point cover embroidered by her sister and herself; and the manager of one of the movie theatres in Saint John had ordered long dark velvet curtains to hang on the wall as background. When Sir James returned, *The Madonna of Port Lligat* (1950) was perfectly in place. Madame Dali (Gala) had been the model for the Madonna.

Even the briefest account of Jimmy and Christofor Dunn's life together must contain a tribute to Olympia (Mrs. Terence) Kedros, who was always there through good times and bad. Following her husband's death in London, she made her home with her sister — liked and admired by all who knew her.

Sir James Dunn died at *Dayspring* on January 1, 1956. It was a great loss for Lady Dunn. Through the Dunn Foundation, great things were achieved for St. Andrews to perpetuate the memory of Jimmy Dunn, the Bathurst boy — all planned or envisioned by Christofor Dunn. A fire hall and fire engine were provided in 1960. The magnificent skating arena was completed in 1962 and a bowling alley added in 1964. Every year on October 29th, Sir James Dunn's birthday, a huge party for three hundred children was given in the Sir James Dunn arena. The Sir James Dunn High School followed in 1966; two larger fire engines in 1967; a health centre and dental clinic in 1974. There were many other projects such as funding for the Meals-on-Wheels program, and scholarships for students at the Community College or funding for a St. Andrews student who was attending Dalhousie University. The Dunn Foundation has been truly generous to our small town, and our children, the main beneficiaries, should be very grateful.

On June 7, 1963, Marcia Christoforides Dunn married Jimmy Dunn's old friend, Max Aitken, Lord Beaverbrook, at the Epsom Registry Office in England. They lived briefly at *Cherkley,* but Max was ill with cancer and died on June 9, 1964.

Lady Beaverbrook continued to divide her time between *Dayspring* in St. Andrews and *Cherkley* in England until her death in 1994.

Mr. and Mrs. Hayter Reed

Pansy Patch was built in 1912 by Mr. and Mrs. Hayter Reed and resembles a Normandy farmhouse, with a thatched-style roof, one round turret, and small windows. When it was advertised for sale in 1927, it was said to be a copy of early Canadian explorer Jacques Cartier's house in St. Malo, Brittany. The long garden at the rear sloped down to Parr Street, and both house and garden were surrounded by a white picket fence. Pansies grew in two small beds by the front door, while a delightful small formal garden, with a stone well in the middle, separated *Pansy Patch* from *Cory Cottage*, also owned by the Hayter Reeds, and later by their son, the architect Gordon Reed.

Undoubtedly the best-loved person associated with this house is the talented Kate Reed. She has left published writings, letters, and many anecdotes connected with her. The daughter of a Chief Justice of Ontario, John Douglas Armour, and the eldest of eleven children, she was married first to Grosvenor Lowrey, a famous New York patent attorney who represented and became a friend of Thomas Edison. Kate Lowrey entered the immensely varied and lively society of New York in the 1880s and became an authority on antiques as well as a connoisseur of painting.

When her husband died, she returned to Canada and began to advise many wealthy art collectors. One of these was William Cornelius Van Horne. In 1894 Kate Lowrey married Hayter Reed, a former Indian Commissioner, who a few years later became Manager-in-Chief of the C.P.R. hotels. Through her earlier connection with Van Horne and other C.P.R. directors, Kate Reed was given the job of decorating the C.P.R. hotels. She was sent to Britain and continental Europe to buy antiques, paintings, and furnishings. The *Chateau Frontenac* in Quebec City was the first hotel she decorated, followed by all the others — including the *Algonquin* and *The Inn* (which she loved best of all).

Pansy Patch, her own house, was filled with beautiful things. The large, low-ceilinged living room had a huge fireplace with this quotation just below the mantel:

Now faire betyde who here abyde, and merrie may they be,
And faire befalle who in this halle repaire in courtesie.
From morne till nighte, be it darke or bright, we banish dole and dree.
Come sit beside our hearth; 'tis wide for gentle companie.

There were twenty-nine ship models at *Pansy Patch,* and Capt. Maloney came every winter to clean them and make any necessary repairs; in addition, the Reeds had a valuable collection of ships in bottles. Bird cages were also collected, and one special one was a combination of a double glass bowl for goldfish on top of the bird cage. The small bird could fly up inside the bowl and it looked as if fish and bird were together.

Mr. and Mrs. Reed loved visitors, and *Pansy Patch* was always filled with interesting people. Jack Lowrey and his sister Grace Daly (Mrs. Reed's family from her first marriage) visited most summers, as did the Reeds' son Gordon, who stayed at *Cory Cottage.* The lovely trees planted on both sides of Reed Avenue were donated by the Hayter Reeds — hence the name.

Kate Reed died in 1927 at the age of seventy-two. In *The Diverting History of a Loyalist Town* (1932), Miss Grace Helen Mowat wrote thus of Kate Reed (whom she knew well):

Kate Reed.

Notman Photo, McCord Museum

But of all those who have made St. Andrews their temporary home, there is one who will ever be remembered. Known the length and breadth of Canada, yet it seems to us we know her best. She knew us all, shouldered our burdens, corrected our mistakes, laughed delightedly at our jokes, enjoyed our gossip, forgave our shortcomings, shared our joys and woes, gave us confidence in ourselves, told us stories of the outside world, stories of the people she had met, the treasures she had collected. Everyone who knew her has some anecdote to tell. Some story of her irrepressible wit, her impulsive generosity, her understanding sympathy, and her unexpected rebukes. Her garden still blooms on the sunny side of the hill. The trees she planted are budding with the spring. "*Pansy Patch*" still stands on the hillside.

Opposite: Pansy Patch, designed by Charles Sax and built in 1912.

D. Will McKay

Mr. and Mrs. Samuel F. Houston were the next owners of *Pansy Patch,* buying it in 1927, the year of Kate Reed's death. They owned it for ten years. Their daughter Eleanor — Mrs.

Pansy Patch • St. Andrews • New Brunswick • Canada •

We built a little Cottage, and fenced it round about
with quietude and happiness, to keep our troubles out
Though the day be overcast, and though the storms begin
peace and joy, are ours at last, safely there within

All the walls are thankfulness, and all the planks are prayer
faith and trust keep off the rust, that comes of anxious care
Hope's the root that shelters us, from every wind of wrong
and love's own light on the hearth burns bright, to warm us, all day
long

Wrought
with love in every stitch
for my daughter
GRACE LOWREY DALY
Finished at Friendly Hall Sturry Kent England
on the anniversary of her Wedding Day
1910 August 21st 1917.

Kate Reed.

Kate Reed's sampler.

Notman Photo, McCord Museum

L.M.C. Smith of Philadelphia — was a great favourite, and she joined in all the parties, picnics, and sports with other teenagers. However, her elderly parents insisted that not only should she always be driven by their chauffeur but that she also be accompanied by Mademoiselle, her governess.

Mr. H.D. Burns, Chairman of the Bank of Nova Scotia, and Mrs. Burns bought the home from the Houstons in 1937 for $5,000. Their family owned the house until 1960 and spent the summers there. Charles, their eldest son, married Janet Wilson, daughter of Mr. Norman Wilson and Senator Cairine Wilson.

Pansy Patch was owned by Mr. and Mrs. John Gale, of Montreal, from 1960 to 1968. After these Canadian owners, the house again returned to Americans when it was sold to Mr. and Mrs. Allen Balliet of Shippensburg, Pennsylvania, and Machias, Maine. In 1969 the Balliets let the house to Mr. William (Bill) Brailley, from Quebec, and he and his family lived there year-round for several years. The children attended school while Bill Brailley operated the Acadian Kitchens, a candy business and shop on Water Street. It became quite a big operation — they even had a shop on Dominion Square in Montreal — before the venture folded. The Acadian Kitchens are still remembered in St. Andrews: thousands of candy boxes and paper bags, printed with its name, were distributed to every church in the town and used for years at church sales.

The new American buyers of *Pansy Patch* in 1979 were Mr. and Mrs. Michael Lazare, of New Milford, Connecticut. They lived in St. Andrews during the summer months and operated a fascinating business in old maps, prints, books, china, silver, and other antiques. At one time, Michael and Kathleen Lazare were buying out the library of Arthur Guiterman in Vermont. He was a poet during the 1920s who had come from New York to Vermont, where he died. To their amazement, they discovered that his bookplate had the same quotation as the one Kate Reed used on the fireplace at *Pansy Patch* — the house the Lazares then owned. A most satisfying coincidence!

Gordon Reed

The original farmhouse that became *Cory Cottage* was built about 1830 and may have belonged to the Haddock family.

After Mr. and Mrs. Hayter Reed built their own house, *Pansy Patch*, in 1912, they bought and remodelled *Cory Cottage* next door in 1915. It was a delightful small house with low ceilings and was beautifully furnished. Two small bay windows were filled with model ships in bottles. The small garden between the two houses had a brick walk and two white wooden benches with high backs; the well at the centre had a graceful wrought iron cupola over it. Pansies and sweet-scented rock plants gave the garden colour and charm. On the other side of the house, there was a small barn which had a curious, large, painted sign above the door, depicting a white horse with mane and tail flying, and below, in big black letters, the following verse:

> Up the hill press me not,
> Down the hill trot me not.
> On the level spare me not,
> In the stable forget me not.

Its origin is uncertain, but a variation of the verse appeared in the *American Horsewoman* (1884) by Elizabeth Karr.

In the summer of 1927, there was much excitement in St. Andrews when Irene Castle, the famous dancer, rented *Cory Cottage* from Gordon Reed. Irene and her husband, Vernon Castle, were a famous exhibition ballroom dancing team between 1911 and 1916 and had helped to popularize the one-step, the tango, and especially the Castle walk. They danced in Paris, London, and New York, as well as in many revues and films. Irene Castle was

Irene Castle at Cory Cottage with her daughter, 1927. Private Collection

recognized as a fashion innovator with enormous influence — particularly with her bobbed hair and split skirts. Vernon Castle, an Englishman by birth, joined the Royal Flying Corps in 1914 and was killed in 1918 in a plane crash.

Much later, Mrs. Castle married Frederick McLaughlin which resulted in a stormy marriage with many ups and downs. So it was as Irene McLaughlin that she came to St. Andrews, bringing her small daughter, Barbara, with her. She also brought a pet mongoose. Always passionate about animals, she had opened her first animal shelter for stray dogs and cats in Deerfield, Illinois, in 1928, naming it "Orphans of the Storm."

St. Andrews people were a little timorous about the mongoose. When Irene Castle (as most people knew her) went shopping with the mongoose draped over her shoulder, the animal would often snap at passersby.

But what lovely dancing there was that summer at the Casino! Everyone wanted to see Irene Castle, and of course all the men wanted to dance with her. Gordon Reed, a friend and a good dancer, was always there, while Mr. Parkin, the hotel manager, fancied himself on the dance floor and thought he was in heaven with Irene Castle. That summer, too, Irene Castle took part in Miss Grace Mowat's Folk Lore Festival, organized for several summers at *Beech Hill*, Miss Mowat's own house. The young men dancers, wearing their large straw hats, had the time of their lives stepping it out on the old wooden platform with one of the most famous dancers in the world.

When the day came in late August for Irene Castle to leave St. Andrews, she intended to depart by the four p.m. train. But early in the afternoon it was discovered that the mongoose was missing. Word went out quickly and soon almost everybody in the town was searching for it. A sixteen-year-old girl located the animal on the croquet lawn just across from the side entrance to the *Algonquin Hotel*. She tried to pick it up, but the mongoose showed its teeth and drove her back. She knew there was little time left, so she dashed into the hotel and breathlessly explained the situation to Mr. Parkin. He grabbed a pair of leather gloves and intrepidly returned with her to the croquet lawn — almost as frightened as the girl but realizing how marvellous it would be to deliver the mongoose to Irene. He seized it up by its tail, and somehow he and the girl reached the station, where a large crowd was saying goodbye to the Castle family. With drama and delight, the beloved beast was restored to its doting mistress, and Mr. Parkin enjoyed one glorious moment.

All the same, he might have mentioned that the girl had spotted it first!

Gordon Reed, owner of *Cory Cottage*, was an architect who inherited many of his mother's artistic gifts. In St. Andrews he was the architect for the Delmar Leighton house; for his own house on Water Street, later owned by Gordon Shirres; and for the Lyndon Dodge house on Joe's Point Road. This had been Mrs. Sarah Childs's very small dwelling — so he literally built the new house around it. The house was later owned by Harrison McCain, of the frozen food empire, and Mrs. Marion McCain, and it remains in the family. Mr. and Mrs. Robert Struthers also had Gordon Reed design many alterations to their Water Street place, formerly the Wheelock Ayscough house.

Gordon Reed had a great eye for colour, and all his houses were beautifully decorated. Someone asked old Mac MacFarlane, the best painter at that time, "How do you ever match these lovely soft colours Mr. Reed uses?" His reply was, "Well, I tell you what I do. I get as close as I can to the colour, and then I paint Mr. Reed's sample — he never knows."

Gordon Reed remained a bachelor until 1937, when he married Marion Graham Ramsey.

Irene Castle dancing with local men at Miss Mowat's Folk Lore Festival, at Beech Hill, 1927. Private Collection

They had one daughter, called Kate. She used to come with her nanny in the summers, sometimes staying at *Cory Cottage*. But Gordon and Marion Reed had a charming house which he had built at St. Sauveur des Monts, and Marion had a very successful interior decorating business, so they made only occasional visits to St. Andrews.

Gordon Reed died in 1959 at the age of sixty-four, whereupon Marion Reed sold both the Water Street house and *Cory Cottage*. These homes were owned for a time by Mrs. Shelagh Robinson and by Judge John F. Kelly of Cohoes, New York, respectively.

The garden at Cory Cottage.

Private Collection

Norman Gregor Guthrie

Mr. and Mrs. Guthrie built *Croix Crest* in 1925. The upper and lower verandahs both over-looked the long narrow garden and St. Andrews harbour beyond. They had owned a much smaller house down at the corner of Mary and Waters streets. Bought in 1904-1905, it once belonged to the Shirley family, but after spending many summers there, the Guthrie family had grown and more space was needed, so that house was torn down when they built *Croix Crest*.

Norman Guthrie was a lawyer from Ottawa whose firm specialized in corporate and parliamentary law. He was born in 1876 and came from Guelph, Ontario. He married Amy Gordon Smith, from Saint John, in 1902, and they had four children: George, Catherine, John, and Gregor. Mrs. Guthrie had come to St. Andrews with her mother as early as 1892, staying at the *Algonquin Hotel*, one of the three Smith sisters who later brought their families to St. Andrews for the summers.

Norman Guthrie was also a poet of quality. As a serious lawyer, however, he evidently felt it necessary to write his poetry under a pseudonym and chose that of "John Crichton," publishing several volumes, including *Flower and Flame* and *A Vista*, under that name. He was a great admirer of Archibald Lampman, about whose works he published a book, and a close friend of Duncan Campbell Scott, with whom he spent much time in Ottawa. Norman Guthrie was also an enthusiastic and knowledgeable gardener and ornithologist. He loved irises, in particular, and had a great variety at *Croix Crest*, many of which were grown from bulbs given to him by the Experimental Farm in Ottawa for testing in our Maritime climate. He also planted a lilac hedge — of many species and colours — all the way up the side of the garden on Mary Street. The lilac hedge endured, but Norman Guthrie had only four years in which to enjoy the place and garden he loved. He died suddenly of pneumonia in 1929.

Amy Guthrie continued to visit for a few summers. Her daughter, Catherine, however, had married Shirley Woods, of Ottawa, in 1928, and the three Guthrie sons had jobs that did not

allow them much time in the summers. So *Croix Crest* was let to the Allan Magee family, the Guthries' relatives from Montreal.

Croix Crest was bought by Mrs. Sarah Smith, of Waterbury, Connecticut, in June 1938. She had first come to St. Andrews with her husband in 1915 and remembered how much she liked it. After his death, she returned to stay with her sister, Miss Margaret Miller, and bought the attractive house.

The father of these two sisters had owned the Mueller Brass Works in Waterbury, and Mrs. (Sally) Smith's husband, Ralph, had either owned or run the steel "mines" there. Mrs. Smith was known as "Fabulous Sal" to her close friends, because of her great generosity. She was extremely wealthy, as was her sister. One of their friends wrote that despite possessing business sense and receiving sound financial advice, they really had too much money for their own good.

When she bought *Croix Crest*, Mrs. Smith tried to leave the house as close to the original plan as possible, with many small bedrooms upstairs. During their time there, the sisters each had a large Packard car with its own chauffeur — George Eggleton and Neil Lorenzon (a Dane). They rented *O'Sea*, later David Coughey's house, and the *Doll House*, later Rose McKay's home, for the chauffeurs. *Invernenty*, later Miss Alice Coughey's house, was rented for guests. Miss Miller also rented Gordon Reed's house on Water Street. She had her own black cook and houseman. Mrs. Smith, who was diabetic, stayed at *Croix Crest* with her own staff and her nurse companion, Mrs. Lyons.

There seemed no end to the houses they needed. In time, Mrs. Smith rented the Henry McQuoid cottage on Chamcook Lake, where she and her sister loved to picnic. When they felt they needed a larger vegetable garden, they bought the Hunt house on Parr Street near the McAleenans. The house was modernized, and Andrew McAleenan became the gardener.

The Kiwanis Club sponsored flower shows in those days, and most of the big cottage gardens competed. Mrs. Smith competed eagerly. Jamie Coughey and Andy McAleenan were proud to win "over all" once, and second prize several times. But they also wondered what their friends thought of two gardeners in two seven-passenger Packards bringing all the flowers and vegetables to the shows! Mrs. Smith liked to give the flowers and vegetables away. When the lilac hedge at *Croix Crest* needed trimming, Jamie Coughey would cut huge bunches of the eight varieties and would deliver them all round the town to friends, stores, churches — and so on. Jamie said: "It must have been a sight for tourists to see me delivering

Opposite: Croix Crest, built in 1925.
Private Collection

*The house owned by Mr. and Mrs. N.G.
Guthrie which was torn down in 1925.*

D. Will McKay

them on my bicycle. I had a garden rake over my shoulder and nearly a hundred pounds of lilacs."

Mrs. Smith was always on the lookout for new places to buy. She bought Bar Island (off Leonardville on Deer Island) and renovated a house there. When visiting some friends on Campobello, she bought two properties (*Down Along* and *Up Along*), hiring Mr. Arthur Mitchell to look after them and make them over. And when Arthur was asked to find an old boat for them to buy, he discovered what had once been quite a famous cargo sailing vessel. Mrs. Smith had this hauled up on the beach on Campobello and cemented in. Three men were hired to rig it up as it used to be — with the addition of red canvas cushions to sit upon. On this landlocked boat the good ladies held their picnic teas for their St. Andrews friends. There were even decorative sails — and if the wind did not blow, a fan provided sufficient breeze. Mrs. T.J. Coughey, Mrs. Jennie Hare, Mrs. D.W. McKay, and Mrs. Edward Maxwell were often present at these picnics.

Not only did the two sisters own real estate in New Brunswick, they also had two large properties in Waterbury, their permanent home. In all, Mrs. Smith probably owned over forty houses. Thirteen were at Schroon Lake, New York (near Ticonderoga). Jamie and Betty Coughey of St. Andrews visited there as guests several times and well remembered, many years later, the huge master bedroom in the largest of those houses where they stayed.

Mrs. Smith and Miss Miller loved beautiful things. They helped many young artists and potters, being particularly fond of New Brunswick's Deichmann pottery and becoming good friends with Kjeld and Erica Deichmann, travelling back and forth between St. Andrews and Moss Glen on the Kingston Peninsula, where the Deichmanns had their pottery. Once when the Deichmanns were giving a demonstration at the Rockefeller Center in New York, Mrs. Smith sent them two tickets for the Metropolitan Opera and money for an excellent dinner. She also mailed them a cheque every Christmas.

With so many places to administer, Sally Smith would lie in bed each morning in St. Andrews writing cheques and instructions to her numerous helpers. Mrs. Lyons, her companion for so many years, gave her staunch support. Mrs. Smith was constantly writing to friends, often with detailed instructions for travelling to places she had procured for them. She also paid for two of her chauffeur's sons to go to Harvard.

Sally Benton Miller Smith and her sister did many thoughtful and generous things for the people of St. Andrews. Unfortunately, they found it hard to get to know, or even to be acknowledged by, the fashionable cottage crowd who were so closely knit. What a lot the cottage crowd missed! We meet so few true originals in life, and fewer still as kind as this — for all their eccentricities.

The house of Edward Maxwell, designed by Maxwell himself and built in 1899. D. Will McKay

Edward Maxwell

Edward Maxwell built his own house in St. Andrews in 1899 and called it *Tillietudlem*, the name of a small Scottish castle once owned by the Maxwell family. As a young architect, he had been brought to St. Andrews by Sir William Van Horne to rectify some of *Covenhoven*'s construction problems. When this was accomplished and he was boarding the train at the Bar Road station, Sir William pointed out a fine property nearby and suggested that Edward Maxwell buy it. It was a beautiful site with five acres of land right at the end of Bar Road and a clear view of Minister's Island and the Bay beyond. He bought it and built *Tillietudlem* that very year. He was thirty-five years of age then and obviously never envisaged that his architectural firm would design so many fine houses in St. Andrews.

Edward Maxwell was born in Montreal on December 31, 1867. His father had been a builder and then a lumber merchant, founding the E.J. Maxwell Lumber Company. Edward attended Montreal High School before he began training in the office of A.F. Dunlop, a Montreal architect, at the age of fifteen. At that time, architecture in the United States was capturing the imagination of Canadians, and many commissions for buildings in Montreal and Toronto went south of the border. Edward Maxwell therefore decided to extend his training in the United States and joined the well-known firm of H.H. Richardson, in Brookline, Massachusetts, later transferring to Shepley, Rutan and Coolidge. Around 1889 he also attended classes at the Boston Architectural Club. But most of his skills were derived directly from his employment.

When the Montreal Board of Trade wished to erect new premises, the president toured the United States and decided that only an American architect could do the job well. Five Americans were therefore asked to submit designs, with Mr. R.M. Hunt, the dean of American architects, as the judge. Quebec architects were of course enraged; they wanted Canadians to be allowed to compete on the same terms, with a Canadian to assist in the judging. The Board refused and local architects declined to enter a competition they believed to be rigged.

The Maxwell Partnership

1902 William Maxwell joined Edward Maxwell

1903 They practised as E. & W.S. Maxwell

1923 Edward Maxwell died

1924 Maxwell & Pitts began practising

Compiled by France Gagnon Pratte, author of *Country Houses for Montrealers, 1892-1924: The Architecture of E. and W.S. Maxwell.*

Summer Homes Designed by Maxwell in St. Andrews

1889 *Tillietudlem*, Bar Road (#56). Owner: Edward Maxwell

1901 *Dalmeny*, Bar Road (#54). Owner: William Hope

1905 *Hillcrest*, Prince of Wales Street (#4). Owner: Charles R. Hosmer

1907 *Rosemount*, Prince of Wales Street (#5). Owner: Charles F. Smith

1909 *Meadow Lodge*, Harriet Street and Prince of Wales Street (#1). Owner: F.W. Thompson

1910 *Cliffside*, Top of King Street (now *Les Goélands*) (#6). Owner: F.H. Markey

1913 Reed Avenue (#30). Owner: O.R. Macklem

1918-1924 *Linkscrest*, Brandy Cove Road (#42). Owner: Sir Thomas Tait

1924 *Derry Bay*, Joe's Point Road (#35). Owner: G. Horne Russell

1930 De Monts Road (#13). Owner: Robert Dodd

Shepley, Rutan and Coolidge were awarded the contract in 1890, and in view of the bad feeling against Americans, it was decided that Edward Maxwell, a Montrealer, would be the most suitable person to supervise the work. It was a golden opportunity for a young architect; he soon attracted attention — and Montreal contracts for himself — by his zeal and hard work. When his employers raised objections, he pointed out that the Board of Trade commission was not suffering and offered to resign if they were displeased. They conceded the point and his practice grew.

Upon completion of the Board of Trade building, Edward Maxwell set up his own office within it and continued his practice in Montreal. At first his work showed very clearly the nature of his training, since his first major commissions — the Henry Birks & Sons store on St. Catherine's Street; the Bell Telephone Company building and the Merchants Bank of Halifax, both on Notre Dame Street — looked very like the work of Shepley, Rutan and Coolidge. The practice grew steadily over more than a decade. In 1902, Edward Maxwell's brother, William S. Maxwell, who had trained in Paris for several years, became his partner. William was particularly successful at winning large architectural competitions, and the reputation of E. and W.S. Maxwell spread widely. Edward Maxwell became an Academician of the Royal Canadian Academy in 1908 and received many other honours.

In 1896, Edward Maxwell married Elizabeth E. Aitchison, an American, and they had four children: Blythe, Jean, Sterling, and Elizabeth. With the growth of this family there was ample excuse to build a new wing on his beloved house in St. Andrews; indeed, several additions were made. In 1988, when a new owner was making major alterations to *Tillietudlem*, one of the workmen came across some rough boards in the attic still bearing the name of a fish-packing firm. How could such a famous architect use such inferior material? Of course, in 1899, when Edward Maxwell built the first version of his cottage, he was not a rich man.

Edward Maxwell's success as an architect was based upon two factors. The first was Canada's expansion and general prosperity at the turn of the century and the second was his understanding of people. He had the gift of forming friendships with those for whom he built houses. And men liked working for him. Wright McLaren, a well-known contractor in St. Andrews, worked for Maxwell on every house he built here. Could there be a better testimonial?

The Maxwell firm did more than design houses; they also designed furniture for many interiors and landscaped gardens. In fact, they had so many commissions to build country houses outside Montreal that in 1908 Edward Maxwell decided to build himself another country house at Baie d'Urfé. It was called *Maxwellton* and had sixty acres of farm and orchard. Here he could be close to his clients when he supervised the construction of their summer cottages. Changes were also made to *Tillietudlem* — an oval dining room was added and a mural was painted above the fireplace. Much later, in 1921, lovely wrought-iron gates, believed to have come from Ireland, were installed.

Edward Maxwell. Private Collection

Despite the appeal of *Maxwellton*, the family continued to spend their summers in St. Andrews — perhaps Baie d'Urfé was just too close to Montreal — though Edward Maxwell was inevitably away from home a great deal. He died in 1923, at the age of fifty-six, when he was working on the reconstruction of the *Chateau Frontenac* in Quebec. However, he is not only remembered in St. Andrews for his beautiful houses, but because he brought a family which became part of the town's life. Grandchildren, great-grandchildren, and great-great-grandchildren followed — five generations of St. Andrews Maxwells.

Mrs. Maxwell was a quiet and gentle person who continued to visit St. Andrews with her children each summer after her husband's death. They were a hospitable family with plenty of guests sailing or playing tennis on their grass court. The Maxwells had a mooring right below the house, and they also swam in the very cold water just opposite the entrance to *Tillietudlem*. The perennial borders in the garden were very beautiful and seemed to have a special brightness — perhaps because they were so close to the sea. When the land was purchased in 1899, there was either a clause in the deed or an unwritten agreement that the fresh water spring near the entrance to the property would always be free and available to the townspeople. This understanding was always honoured by the Maxwells. Even after the gates were closed, a small path was left open to the spring.

After Mrs. Edward Maxwell died, *Tillietudlem* was owned by her daughter Jean (Mrs. Kenneth Fleming) from Windsor, Ontario. She and her husband came with their children — Marjorie, Jean (Jeffie), and Maxwell (Max). Jean Fleming was very proud of the fact that she spent seventy-eight summers there. Other grandchildren of Mr. and Mrs. Edward Maxwell visited *Tillietudlem* from time to time, but it was the Fleming family that knew it best.

Jeffie Fleming married Sydney Woodd-Cahusac and moved to Connecticut. Among her delightful memories of childhood, she recalled the thrill of being old enough to walk up alone to the Bar Road Station to collect the mail from the train. When the tide was off the Bar, the

**Town Houses Designed by
Maxwell in St. Andrews**

1900 The Presbyterian manse,
Greenock Church, Elizabeth Street

1910 Montague Street
Owner: Edwin O'Dell

Plans for Alterations

1898 *Fort Tipperary,* Prince of Wales
Street (#3), plans never used.
Owner: Lord Shaughnessy then
Thomas Shaughnessy

1899 *Covenhoven,* Minister's Island
(#57).
Owner: Sir William Van Horne

1904 King Street. Owner: F. McColl
Frederick Street.
Owner: John O'Neill

1915 De Monts Road (#16).
Owner: Robert Gill

1943 De Monts Avenue (#13).
Owner: Lady Davis

≈≈≈≈≈≈≈≈≈≈≈≈≈≈≈≈≈≈≈≈≈

children used to hide in the bushes near the railway tracks in the hope that Billy Van Horne would make one of his mad dashes in a fast car across the Bar and up the hill. They hoped to see him cut in front of the train with a split second to spare!

The Fleming children had an old-fashioned nanny, as other families did in those days. Nanny and the Fleming's cook used to invite their friends out from St. Andrews for tea. One of these friends recalls an occasion when the children failed to come straight in from their play in the garden and Nanny stood up shouting: "If you don't come straight away, I'll have your guts for garters!" Can you imagine what child specialists would say about that today? But, then, they probably wouldn't know what garters were.

When Mrs. Fleming died, *Tillietudlem* was left to her son Maxwell. He sold it in 1983 to John Shaw, a well-known potter from Ontario. He built a kiln in the old stable and made further improvements before the property was again sold in 1986 — to Mr. J.C. Gregorie, from the United States.

Charles R. Hosmer

Charles Randolph Hosmer and Mrs. Hosmer built this large summer cottage, with its commanding view of the town of St. Andrews, in 1905. Edward Maxwell designed the house, its furniture, and the garden. At the rear, the verandahs look out onto spacious lawns and flower gardens, with Minister's Island and Passamaquoddy Bay in the distance. Edward Dougherty was the gardener for many years.

Born in Coteau Landing, Quebec, in 1851, Charles Hosmer married Clara Jane Bigelow. They had one son, Elwood Bigelow Hosmer, and a daughter, Olive. Charles had left school at the age of fourteen and studied telegraphy with the Grand Trunk Railway. A year later he was put in charge of the telegraph office. He joined the Dominion Telegraph Company, where he became Superintendent in 1873 at the age of twenty-two. His final move was to the C.P.R., where he was appointed Head of the Telegraph Department in January 1886, when he was thirty-five.

Charles Hosmer. Notman Photo, McCord Museum

Thirteen years later he retired from the C.P.R. a rich man — and would become even more so. He was the founder and first President of the Ogilvie Flour Mills Company and also became a director of the Bank of Montreal and twenty-six other companies, as well as a governor of the three largest hospitals in Montreal. The Hosmers had a large and opulent house on Drummond Street in Montreal, filled with beautiful things, especially a fine collection of paintings, which included four Canalettos, said to be among the very finest. With the exception of the Canalettos, most of the Hosmer collection now belongs to the Beaverbrook Art Gallery in Fredericton.

When H.R.H the Prince of Wales visited Montreal in the 1920s, Charles Hosmer gave a magnificent ball in the Prince's honour at the Drummond Street house. Miss Marguerite Pillow, daughter of Mr. and Mrs. Howard Pillow, was then still attending Miss Edgar's and Miss Cramp's School for Girls, but she was allowed to attend the ball given by her great-uncle and great-aunt, where she danced with the Prince — a magical evening for a young girl.

Clara Hosmer. D. Will McKay

The Hosmers were kindly and very sociable, with many friends, and travelled widely. Charles Hosmer was particularly known for his liveliness and wit, being interested in the theatre and the arts in general. Nellie Melba, the great opera singer, was a personal friend. Near the end of his life, Charles Hosmer had a stroke, which affected his speech. He came to St. Andrews often then, and every day his chauffeur, Thomas, would take him in a long, black open car on his favourite drive, round and round Indian Point. Then they would stop at the thirteenth hole on the golf course (below what became *Anderson House*), where his golfing friends would stop by and talk to him. When callers came to *Hillcrest*, he had lots of lettered wooden blocks, which he could manipulate very quickly into words and thus communicate with them.

One story about *Hillcrest* must be told. Mr. Clarence Mackay, President of Postal Telegraph and Cable Corporation in the United States, had an attractive daughter named Ellin. She had fallen in love with a young and already prosperous pianist and composer — and he with her. His name was Irving Berlin. Since the young man was Jewish, Clarence Mackay did not approve at all and tried everything to separate the young couple. He and Charles Hosmer were old friends, so in the summer of 1923 he sent Ellin all the way to St. Andrews to stay at *Hillcrest* with the Hosmers. Her suitor followed and proposed marriage. Since Ellin was only

Hillcrest, built in 1905, designed by Edward Maxwell. D. Will McKay twenty and her father so against the union, she was sent abroad for seven months in 1924. But she did not waver. On January 4, 1926, she married Irving Berlin. Ellin died on July 29, 1988, and Irving Berlin on September 22, 1989, at the age of 101. They had been married for sixty-two years.

Before their marriage, Clarence Mackay had declared: "The day you marry my daughter, I will disinherit her" — to which Irving Berlin replied: "The day I marry your daughter, I'll settle a million dollars on her" (he was then worth at least four million). So he called Clarence Mackay's bluff with a vengeance.

Elwood Bigelow Hosmer was born in 1879 and died in 1947 at age sixty-eight. Married for a short time, then divorced, he had no children. He was a short, rather unattractive man who worked occasionally as a stockbroker but spent most of his time travelling, buying paintings, and smoking huge cigars. He was also a perpetual visitor to the Palm Court in the *Ritz Carlton Hotel* in Montreal, where he drank a lot. Sir Andrew McPhail, a physician and man of letters, and Alphonse Jongers, a well-known portrait painter, were boon companions: with Elwood Hosmer, they made three ugly men. Elwood lived at the *Ritz* during the last years of his life. However, he must have had a well-hidden spirit of adventure because in 1927 some friends persuaded him to fly the Atlantic. Unfortunately, his plane — the *Flying Whale* — crashed after taking off from the Azores, and he and his three partners spent twelve hours drifting in the ocean until they were picked up by the liner *Minnewaska*. The newspapers reported that at the time Elwood was found he was sitting on a wing of the plane, calmly reading John Buchan's *Greenmantle*. After this experience, he returned to his armchair in the *Ritz*.

He kept up his interest in flying sufficiently, however, to drive from St. Andrews to Pennfield Ridge in August 1932, when Jim Mollison touched down after his dramatic east-to-west crossing of the Atlantic. Elwood protected him from the Press and brought him back to spend the night at *Hillcrest*.

It was sad that the Hosmers left no grandchildren to inherit the large fortune left by Mr. and Mrs. Charles Hosmer and by Elwood and his sister Olive. There was of course an extended family: Mrs. Hosmer's sister, Mrs. Heney, had a daughter, Marjorie, who married George Shuter — and they had a son and a daughter. Mrs. Heney's son Theodore married Amy Springett — and there were two daughters and a son from this marriage. This extended family benefited greatly from the fortune of the former telegraph boy from Coteau Landing.

Portrait of Elwood Hosmer by Alfred Jongers. Notman Photo, McCord Museum

47

Risford, 1885
Renamed *Penryn*, 1950
Renamed *Tara Manor*, 1971
Mowat Drive

Emery Hoar and C.D. Howe

Prof. and Mrs. John Emery Hoar, of Cambridge, Massachusetts, bought land on Mowat Drive in 1885, where they built their summer house called *Risford*. Prof. Hoar taught at Harvard and was one of the first Americans to own property in St. Andrews. There had been a small house called *Bellevue* on the site since 1871, which had been bought — though not lived in — by Dr. Charles Tupper in that year and sold in 1872. He then purchased the stone house across the road and called it *Highland Hill*. (That property became *Clibrig*, the Wilson estate.)

After Prof. Hoar died, the house was inherited by his son, D. Blakeney Hoar. Blakeney and Mrs. Hoar — the professor's third wife — continued to come to Saint Andrews for many years, until his death in 1922. People remember him as a rather plump, middle-aged man, who drove about the town in an open carriage with his white-haired stepmother. He apparently gained some social stature — there is a "D. Blakeney Hoar Square" in Brookline, Massachusetts.

Risford was left in trust to the executors of the Hoar Estate, and it was used by or let to relatives until 1945, when it was bought by Mr. and Mrs. Lloyd D. Murray. They sold it in 1950 to the Hon. Clarence Decatur Howe and his wife, Alice Martha Howe, who changed the name to *Penryn*. "C.D." (as he was always known) and Mrs. Howe owned *Penryn* until 1961: a very happy period for this lovely estate overlooking Passamaquoddy Bay.

C.D. Howe was born an American but became a Canadian citizen in 1913. Indeed, both he and his wife came from Waltham, Massachusetts. They had two sons and three daughters. It was when C.D. came to Halifax, with a degree from M.I.T., to teach engineering at Dalhousie University from 1908 to 1913, that he established his Canadian connection. In 1913 he readily abandoned the academic life and went to work with the Canadian Board of Grain Commissioners, designing grain elevators across the Prairies — and founding an engineering firm for that purpose. He became pre-eminent in this field, constructing elevators across Canada and in Argentina between 1916 and 1935. When the recession hit his business, he was elected to Parliament as a Liberal in 1935, entering Mackenzie King's cabinet to become Minister of Transport in 1936. His political career reached its peak during the Second World War, when as Minister of Munitions and Supply he took on the task of managing Canada's war production. He succeeded brilliantly with his straightforward, blunt personality, working alongside a group of conservative businessmen who came to appreciate his efficient and daring conduct of economic affairs. In 1944 he presided over the Department of Reconstruction and later filled several other ministerial posts until the controversies concerning the Pipeline Debate of 1956 brought about his downfall and that of the Liberal government in the following year.

Risford, built in 1885, later renamed Penryn by C.D. Howe, and later known as Tara Manor. D. Will McKay

Although he was not able to spend much time in St. Andrews from 1950 to 1961, the town did get to know him. He liked to visit the Old Men's Club, talk to people along the street or at the end of the wharf, and play golf. A rather stern-looking man, he was kind to others. He was one of Canada's great men; a man who got things done, who in his directness and drive was reminiscent of that earlier go-getter, Sir William Van Horne.

Mrs. Alice Howe, a strong, good-looking woman, was a real New Englander, no less a personality in her own right than her husband. Very direct, she managed everything to do with the family and houses. For a short time, the Howes owned two houses in St. Andrews — a large one on Reed Avenue as well as *Penryn*. The Reed Avenue house had been built in 1910 by Mrs. Edward C. Walker, of Walkerville, Ontario, and was later owned by Mr. and Mrs. Guy Murchie. (The Howes would sell it in due course to Mr. and Mrs. Robert Craig of Montreal.) *Penryn* was bought primarily for children and grandchildren. And what a wonderful grandmother they had in Alice Howe! With the assistance of a resident nanny and local help to run the large house, which had spacious grounds to play in and a pony, Mrs. Howe planned all the meals and picked the fresh vegetables herself. She established the routine: meals on time; Katy's Cove for swimming in the mornings; rest in the afternoon; then, after other activities, early to bed. Alice Howe, although very loving and human, was the sort of person who expected to be obeyed — and usually was. She was also an excellent and most

C.D. Howe.

knowledgeable gardener, doing most of the work in the gardens herself. For some years until the early 1970s, when ill health forced her resignation, Alice Howe was an alternate member of the Roosevelt International Park Commission.

C.D. Howe died in 1960. *Penryn* was then sold, and the Howe family went elsewhere for their summers. But they still remembered their happy days in St. Andrews, and several have returned for visits.

Dr. Reid A. Rawding and his wife, Tessa B. Rawding, bought *Penryn* in 1961. Dr. Rawding was a retired dentist from the United States. While both he and his wife were American, they did have a connection with New Brunswick. Their daughter Joan married John Williamson of Fredericton (formerly of St. Andrews) and they later purchased *Pottery Creek* in St. Andrews. In May 1965, *Penryn* was bought by Norman and Sharon Ryall, who converted it six years later into the *Tara Manor Inn & Restaurant*.

Frederick W. Thompson

Mr. Frederick W. Thompson, of Montreal, built this twenty-room shingled residence in 1909. It had a carriage house and stables, with living quarters for the coachman, a lovely garden, tennis courts, and lawns surrounded by a high hedge that was five feet thick in places and took two men most of the summer to clip. (There were no electric clippers in those days.) Edward Maxwell designed the house, the furniture, and also the landscaping for the garden.

Frederick William Thompson was managing director of Ogilvie Flour Mills in Montreal. He had probably been introduced to St. Andrews by Charles R. Hosmer, a founder of Ogilvie Flour Mills, who had his own summer cottage in the town. Mr. and Mrs. Thompson had four children — and later two of their widowed daughters, Mrs. Helen Balfour and Mrs. Alice Wilson, bought *Greenock House* in order to live permanently in St. Andrews. Mrs. Wilhelmina Thompson was herself a widow for forty-two years, and *Meadow Lodge* remained in the family until her death.

Meadow Lodge was always a house of warm hospitality. Three grandsons — David, Fred and Peter Rea– and their sister, Jocelyn, spent most of their summers there with their grandmother during the twenties and thirties with the many other guests. The Rea brothers had a Ford station wagon, one of the early wooden-frame ones. It was nicknamed "Cuthbert" or "Cuthy" and must have called at every house in St. Andrews where there was a pretty daughter. They were a good-looking trio — generally dressed in white flannels and white blazers with their school crest — and won most of the prizes at golf, tennis, and swimming. When Fred Rea looked back after fifty years, he wrote that "Outstandingly happy memories remain with me of a generous, vital, and entertaining Family."

Meadow Lodge was sold in 1963 to Mr. Maxwell Pascal of the Pascal hardware business in Montreal, who renamed the house *Surrey Gardens*. Then in 1966 it was bought by Lady Dunn to accommodate the big-name hockey players and coaches — men like Jacques Plante, Scotty

Bowman, Doug Harvey, and others — who were brought in by Bill O'Neill to the Sir James Dunn Arena. The house was sold again in 1977, this time to Dr. and Mrs. John Findlay of Fredericton. The Findlays restored the name of *Meadow Lodge*, gave the house and grounds the care they needed, and revived the hospitable atmosphere of the Thompson days.

Meadow Lodge, designed by Edward Maxwell (1909). D. Will McKay

Sir Samuel Leonard Tilley and Miss Olive Hosmer

Sir Leonard and Lady Tilley bought *Linden Grange* from Benjamin Stevenson of St. Andrews in 1871. (The original house was built in 1829.) Born in Gagetown, New Brunswick, in 1818, Leonard Tilley was twice married, his second wife being Alice, daughter of Zachariah Chipman of St. Stephen. A member of the New Brunswick Legislative Assembly for many years, Sir Leonard Tilley became one of the Fathers of Confederation and Minister of Customs in the first cabinet of the Dominion of Canada in 1867. He was twice appointed Lieutenant-Governor of New Brunswick, the second term of office lasting until 1893. He died three years later in Saint John.

When the Tilleys bought *Linden Grange* they became the first summer visitors to buy property in St. Andrews. Sir Leonard took a keen interest in the town — as president of both the St. Andrews Land Company, which did much to promote tourism, and the St. Andrews Hotel Company, which financed the building of the *Algonquin Hotel* in 1889.

In 1871 *Linden Grange* was a much smaller house than it is today. The Tilleys made some changes, of course, over their long ownership, but the major changes came later. In 1921 the house was auctioned off from the front steps of the post office (the brick house on Water Street built in 1889 by the St. Andrews Land Company for their offices), and the top bidder was Charles Hosmer, father of Miss Olive Hosmer. She became the new owner, and Hosmer money was quickly applied to *Linden Grange*. The verandahs were enlarged and painted, and a second tower was added at this time. The whole garden was fenced in and landscaped. A special dog run was constructed for Miss Hosmer's miniature Pekinese dogs, of which she had quite a few.

Miss Hosmer was a charming, shy lady who suffered from poor health. Perhaps her parents were overprotective: when she complained about the noise generated by *Elm Corner*, the guest house at the corner of Edward and Carleton streets, her father bought it and tore it down. Since cows grazing at the top of William Street — on the site of what later became

Sir James Dunn Academy — were also known to make noises, Mr. Hosmer bought the field. In addition, the top of William Street was closed to traffic. Nevertheless, Miss Hosmer did have genuine charm. Children liked to be taken to tea with her by their mothers; she seemed to feel at home with them. Thoughtful and generous, she had special winter coats made by Ogulnick of Montreal, an expensive tailor, for the small daughters of friends — and sometimes they even had little mink collars.

Olive Hosmer enjoyed taking chauffeured drives in her four-door convertible; St. George was one of her favourite places. She came every summer to St. Andrews, travelling in one of the C.P.R. private cars, the *Mount Royal*, and accompanied by her household staff and Pekinese, only to return to Montreal in early September — again by the *Mount Royal*. When she died in 1965, she left *Linden Grange* to Mrs. May Spurge, her personal maid and companion for many years. Later that same year it was sold to Mrs. Margaret Jeanne B. Heenan, and since her death, the ownership has remained in the Heenan family. Miss Olive Hosmer left money in her will to the various churches in St. Andrews and to the town to provide playgrounds or sports fields for the children.

Linden Grange, built in 1829. E.H. Snell

George Inness Jr.

Lazy Croft, 1893
Acadia and Prince of Wales Streets
Destroyed by fire, 1972

The second summer cottage to be located in St. Andrews was built in 1893 by George Inness Jr. of New York. An artist and keen yachtsman, he had been born in Paris in 1853 and was forty when he and his wife, née Julia G. Smith, came to St. Andrews. Mrs. Inness was the daughter of Roswell Smith, publisher of *Century Magazine*, and brought her considerable wealth to the marriage. In addition to *Lazy Croft*, they had *Craigsmoor* in Ulster County, New York, and a house in Florida.

Lazy Croft certainly reflected George Inness Jr.'s love of boats — perhaps to its detriment. It was a long, narrow, shingled house, with his studio placed at the "bow" overlooking the Bay. The small bedrooms at the back of the house could only be reached by a narrow outside balcony, like a ship's deck, while downstairs the walls had large rivets in them resembling the inside of a ship. Unfortunately, very little is known about George and Sarah Inness's time in St. Andrews.

Geroge's father, George Inness Sr. was a gifted artist and the subject of an admiring biography by his son, *Life, Art and Letters of George Inness*, published in 1917. His paintings are in many private collections and major galleries in the United States, where he is considered to be one of the leading American painters of his time and his work is prized. Curiously, he did not like to sign his paintings. It was because George Inness Sr. knew Sir William Van Horne that the Inness family first came to St. Andrews. Apart from sharing good times socially, they painted together — and indeed both had paintings entitled *Moonlight on Passamaquoddy Bay*, George Inness Sr.'s being in the Ryerson Collection at the Art Institute in Chicago. In his biography, George Inness Jr. describes the painting of this picture in St. Andrews, when he was himself present. George Inness Sr. died in Scotland in 1894 while on a holiday at Bridge of Allan.

Lazy Croft was not a pretty house. Its long thin shape behind the hedge did not attract attention and its main interest — only really acknowledged in recent years — lay in its

association with the talented Innesses. The house was later bought by Mr. George Hopkins, a wealthy stockbroker from New York. An expert sailor and the commodore of the New York Yacht Club, he had a splendid yacht called *Seiglinde*. Since he and his wife spent many summers in St. Andrews, they did a lot of sailing in Passamaquoddy Bay. They are still remembered for many kindnesses, and for Mr. Hopkins' deep, jolly laugh. Their daughter, Mrs. Hobart Johnson, of Wisconsin, later owned *Lazy Croft*, and it was let for several summers during the fifties and sixties to Thomas Shaughnessy, grandson of Lord Shaughnessy, and his wife, Margot. Their three charming daughters — Amanda, Roxanne, and Tara — spent their childhood summers there, and it was the Shaughnessys who bought the house from the Johnson family, only for it to burn down in 1972.

Lazy Croft, the cottage of George Inness Jr., built by Stevenson & Mackenzie of St. Stephen in 1893. D. Will McKay

Charles F. Smith

5

Rosemount, 1907
Prince of Wales Street

Charles F. Smith, of Montreal, had his large summer cottage built next door to that of C.R. Hosmer in 1907. *Rosemount* was an Edward Maxwell house for which he designed the interior, furniture, and garden, in addition to the main building.

Charles Smith was born in Aldershot, England, in 1841 and came to Canada first in 1861 with his regiment, the 62nd Foot. This was at the time of the American Civil War when the British government sent out a large number of troops to Quebec and New Brunswick. The 62nd Regiment landed at Gove's Cove in St. Andrews on December 30, 1861, Gove's large warehouses having been converted into barracks. St. Andrews was an ice-free port, of course, and the steamer *Delta*, owned by Cunard, had carried the troops through very rough seas. The soldiers remained in St. Andrews until January 1, 1862, when 153 men were sent each day by rail to Canterbury, New Brunswick. The railway ended there and the soldiers then travelled on to Woodstock by sleigh. According to Charles F. Smith's account (as recalled by his daughter, Gerry Hampson) the regiment then proceeded to Fredericton and on to Rivière-du-Loup by sleigh or snowshoe, encountering severe blizzards en route.

When the regiment returned to England, Charles F. Smith retired from the Army and returned to Canada. He bought the leather firm of Ames Holder McCready in Montreal and became a director. It was much later, when he had become a friend of Charles Hosmer and Sir William Van Horne, that he returned to St. Andrews. Perhaps, as a young soldier in 1861, he had walked over the very land where as a rich man he would build his beautiful *Rosemount* forty-six years later.

The Smiths had one son, Charles F., and four daughters, including Rose (Mrs. Doyle) — who often spent summers in St. Andrews — and Geraldine (Gerry), Mrs. R.H. Hampson of Ottawa, who described their St. Andrews summers in a charming letter. In those days they brought their horses and carriages from Montreal by train — a single horse for the morning carriage and a pair for the afternoon. They also brought a staff of servants. Gerry Hampson

recalled that, after the train journey from Montreal, the cook was not expected to provide lunch. This was sent over from *Elm Corner* by Miss Susan Mowat and Miss Annie Campbell. Mrs. Hampson could still remember and almost taste the lemon tarts after more than sixty years.

In later years, *Rosemount* was bought by Edward MacKay, of Montreal, and he and his family spent many summers there. His daughter, Mrs. Anna Reay Cundill, inherited *Rosemount* but sold it in 1955 to the Hosmer Estate. The house was beautifully maintained and cared for. Mr. amd Mrs. Murray Vaughan's son, David, and daughter, Lucinda, spent many summers there with their families. Lucinda and her husband, John Flemer, continued to come there for summers, and this large house with its spacious grounds has delighted many visitors.

Rosemount, designed by Edward Maxwell and built in 1907. D. Will McKay

F.H. Markey and A. Murray Vaughan

6

Cliffside, 1910
Remodelled as *Les Goélands*, 1951
Top of King Street

A lawyer from Montreal, Mr. F.H. Markey built his long, narrow summer cottage at the top of King Street, with a superb view of the Bay. He and his wife, Laura, a large and cheerful lady, had two sons — Henry and Donald — who spent most of their summers in St. Andrews during the twenties and thirties. They were both drivers of fast cars, but it is remembered that their father before them had ridden in a fine carriage with high-stepping horses.

When Mr. and Mrs. Murray Vaughan, of Montreal and Toronto, bought the Markey house in 1951, they remodelled it almost completely, renaming it *Les Goélands*. It was a most attractive house, with beautifully landscaped grounds, a modern swimming pool, and a delightful walled garden at the rear. The flowering shrubs and well-kept hedges and lawns

Cliffside, designed by Edward Maxwell and built in 1910. Private Collection

made one of the finest gardens in the town. Marguerite Vaughan was a most knowledgeable gardener and did much of the gardening herself in the early years.

Murray Vaughan was born in Saint John in 1899. He first came to St. Andrews as a young bachelor in 1923 but soon after he went on to Montreal, where he was with the Bank of Montreal and later with Eastern Securities. He was a tall, good-looking man, with prematurely greying hair, inevitably nicknamed "The Silver Fox" in his early thirties. His ambition was to make a lot of money and marry a rich and beautiful girl. He succeeded spectacularly when he and Marguerite Pillow were married in Montreal in 1934. She was the only child of Mr. and Mrs. Howard Pillow, of Montreal. The Vaughans would later celebrate their fiftieth wedding anniversary in St. Andrews.

Murray Vaughan joined the British American Bank Note Company in 1940. In later years he became President and then Chairman. In 1969 he was made a Companion of the Order of Canada for his support of the arts in Canada, in particular the Musée des Beaux-Arts in Montreal. He and his wife were great benefactors of St. Andrews in many different ways. Sunbury Shores Arts & Nature Centre has been a special interest to their family. The Vaughans also restored the lovely old brick house on King Street known as the *Hibbard House* and gave it to the Province of New Brunswick. Furthermore, when plans were made to build

Cliffside, remodelled as Les Goélands by A. Murray Vaughan, 1951. Private Collection

Passamaquoddy Lodge, a senior citizens' home in St. Andrews, the Vaughans generously gave the land. Murray Vaughan also paid for many improvements in the St. Andrews Rural Cemetery — the old iron gates were repaired, more help was hired for caretaking, and the older tombstones were cleaned and reset. The Vaughans' generosity to the Beaverbrook Gallery and to the University of New Brunswick is well known; their Tecolote Foundation is named after the Mexican word for owl, since Marguerite Vaughan collected paintings, carvings, and sculptures of owls. When you are rich it is perhaps less difficult to give money away. But Murray and Marguerite Vaughan are remembered in St. Andrews not only for their benefactions but also because they gave caring advice and support when it was needed.

Murray Vaughan died in St. Andrews on July 19, 1986, at age eighty-seven. The Vaughans' two children, Lucinda and David, spent their childhood summers in the town, continued to visit, staying at *Rosemount*, the house next door to *Les Goélands*. The six grandchildren also visit, and there are now great-grandchildren representing the fifth St. Andrews generation.

Marguerite Vaughan was remarried in November 1987 to Dr. Joseph Eller, and for a time they lived in Palm Beach, Florida. Dr. Eller died in February 1989, and Marguerite Vaughan in 1991.

The Shaughnessy Family at Fort Tipperary

Sir Thomas and Lady Shaughnessy built *Fort Tipperary*, their summer cottage, in 1902. It was situated on the site of the original Fort built to house the British garrison during the War of 1812.

Research has not revealed the name of Sir Thomas' architect, though he may have been a member of the C.P.R. staff. Edward Maxwell did do some drawings for Sir Thomas but they were not used for *Fort Tipperary*. When the house was built the old wooden buildings of the Fort were taken down; however, the grass-covered ramparts remained as well as the ancient black cannon. *Fort Tipperary* is a large house with spacious gardens overlooking Passamaquoddy Bay and Minister's Island.

Thomas George Shaughnessy was born in Milwaukee in 1853. Although an American, he was to become a great Canadian. He married Elizabeth Bridge Nagle, also from Milwaukee, in 1880.

Entering railway work at the age of sixteen, Thomas Shaughnessy went on to serve in the purchasing department of the Chicago-Milwaukee & St. Paul Railroad, the company that William Van Horne left to join the C.P.R. Van Horne soon realized that he needed Thomas Shaughnessy and offered him the job of chief purchasing agent for the C.P.R. Reluctant at first, Shaughnessy was finally persuaded.

In 1882, Thomas Shaughnessy was certainly Van Horne's most notable recruit. He was only twenty-nine years of age and something of a dandy in the way he dressed. While his special qualities were not immediately apparent to everyone, the C.P.R. soon knew that his appointment was second only to that of Van Horne himself.

During the mad dash of construction across the Prairies and through the Rockies, supplies were of the greatest importance. The year 1885 proved a particularly dramatic one for Van Horne and the railway. Though the financial situation was desperate, Thomas Shaughnessy, a

Opposite: Lord and Lady Shaughnessy at Fort Tipperary with family and friends.

Private Collection

T.G. Shaughnessy (Lord Shaughnessy, Baron Shaughnessy of Montreal and Ashford). C.P.R.

man of cool common sense, never appeared to show the slightest tremor of panic. He just kept on juggling bills, cheques, notes of credit, promises, and threats, in order to keep Van Horne supplied with the cash he needed and the supplies the construction teams had to have.

Thomas Shaughnessy was a company man through and through, with few interests outside his work. While William Van Horne and his cronies were playing poker, Thomas Shaughnessy preferred solitaire, which he played night after night — all the time working out business details in his mind. He had few close associates, and when he became President of the C.P.R. in 1899, he installed his own elevator at the office. He did not want any employee to share it with him. Austere in manner and a strict disciplinarian, he was nevertheless abso-lutely fair to those who worked for him and quick to recognize and reward merit. His own case certainly set an example. Thomas Shaughnessy had saved the C.P.R. from bankruptcy and served as President until he retired in 1918. He was knighted in 1901 and made a Knight Commander of the Victorian Order in 1907.

Dramatic and major changes took place during his presidency at the C.P.R. From 1899 to 1918 came the first large-scale immigration to the Prairies, and the C.P.R. also grew enor-mously. Its mileage of track grew from 7,739 to 13,772 during the period when Sir Thomas was President, and gross earnings grew from $29,230,000 to $157,357,000. Meanwhile, the company enlarged itself in other ways. The acquisition of a smelter and mines in northern British Columbia and their development by the Consolidated Mining & Smelting Co. (later COMINCO) was another achievement. But the venture Sir Thomas apparently enjoyed most was the inauguration of a steamship service on the Atlantic Ocean, similar to the one Van Horne had established for the Pacific.

An introspective man who tended to shy away from publicity, Sir Thomas left "public relations" — including tourism promotion — to employees whom he appointed personally. The most influential "image-maker" for the C.P.R. was an Oxford graduate and freelance writer from Fleet Street named John Murray Gibbon. He was given his first assignment by Sir Thomas Shaughnessy in 1907; it was to line up twelve leading British newspaper editors to tour Canada as guests of the President of the C.P.R. Arriving in Quebec, they spent eight weeks travelling across the country, and the tour was a tremendous success.

The C.P.R.'s first Atlantic fleet had been acquired by purchasing the Elder Dempster Line. But its fifteen ships were small and undistinguished. Sir Thomas moved quickly to upgrade the service. Two luxurious liners, capable of eighteen knots, were ordered to be built on the

Firth of Clyde in Scotland, and the vessels went into service in 1906 as the *Empress of Britain* and the *Empress of Ireland*.

Murray Gibbon's new slogan for the C.P.R. was "Canadian Pacific, World's Greatest Travel System," and Sir Thomas Shaughnessy's Atlantic campaign was crowned in 1909 with the purchase of the Allan Line, though the agreement was not made public until six years later. The two lines continued to operate independently; when they did formally amalgamate, they first became Canadian Pacific Ocean Services and then, in 1921, Canadian Pacific Steamships Ltd.

During the First World War, the C.P.R. made an enormous commitment of ships, personnel, facilities, and material, but every civilian branch of the company suffered. This was accepted with equanimity. Unfortunately, the expected postwar recovery failed to happen. Sir Thomas Shaughnessy had of course been at the centre of the C.P.R.'s war efforts, and his work in transportation and financing led to him being named Baron Shaughnessy of Montreal and Ashford in 1916. His resignation as company President in 1918 was hastened by failing eyesight, though he remained — like Sir William Van Horne before him — as Chairman of the Board until his death in 1923. The new President was Edward Wentworth Beatty.

The two C.P.R. presidents who chose St. Andrews as their summer home could not have been more different: Sir William was an extrovert, a driver of men, while Lord Shaughnessy was austere and shy, although a brilliant manager. At the end of his career it was said of Lord Shaughnessy that he was undoubtedly the greatest railway administrator in the world.

Lord and Lady Shaughnessy had a very large house in Montreal on Dorchester Street West (later the Canadian Centre for Architecture), which they left each summer to travel to *Fort Tipperary*, usually in their private railway car, the *Killarney*. In St. Andrews, Lord Shaughnessy could abandon some of his cares and relax with his family about him. He liked a game of golf, although caddies remembered him as a difficult customer. He also enjoyed sailing and chartered a yacht called the *Maple Leaf*, of which Capt. Howard Rigby was the master.

The Shaughnessys were very generous about entertaining; any important visitor to St. Andrews was invited to *The Fort*. There were garden parties and endless tea parties. With their three daughters, Alice, Marguerite, and Edith (Bud), there were always lots of young people around enjoying the summer activities. The Shaughnessy family members were almost all musical and had the wonderful Irish capacity for entertaining themselves and others. They loved to dress up, to act, to dance, and to take part in masquerade balls. This tendency

Capt. the Hon. Alfred Shaughnessy, son of Sir Thomas Shaughnessy. CPR

towards the music hall, the stage, and towards dressing up was evident even into the fifth generation.

When the First World War came, tragedy struck the Shaughnessy family as it did so many others. Capt. the Hon. Alfred Shaughnessy, who went overseas with the 60th Battalion, was killed in action in 1916. He was the Shaughnessy's youngest son.

Lord Shaughnessy died on December 10, 1923, after a very brief illness. The funeral was held on the 13th at St. Patrick's Church (later St. Patrick's Cathedral) at ten a.m. At that hour, trains throughout the entire C.P.R. system, the ships at sea, and all C.P.R. activities were halted for two minutes.

Lady Shaughnessy continued to summer in St. Andrews, with her daughter, the Hon. Marguerite Shaughnessy, after her husband's death. She was truly a remarkable woman, who kept pace with her husband all the way. Married young, in Milwaukee, she could hardly have imagined what the future would hold. But she managed everything: five children, an imposing house in Montreal, and *Fort Tipperary*. Travelling abroad with her eminent husband, she had attended many important functions; at home she met and entertained members of the Royal Family and countless other distinguished guests. But the Baroness was still the young woman from Milwaukee, and her family, in particular, remembered her for her quiet sense of humour.

Lady Shaughnessy died in May 1937, and although the funeral service was held in Montreal, a mass was also celebrated in the St. Andrews Roman Catholic Church.

The Hon. Marguerite Shaughnessy inherited *Fort Tipperary* after her mother's death and continued to stay there for summers until 1942, when she decided to take up permanent residence in St. Andrews. She was the first of the summer visitors to take that important step.

Though *The Fort* was fine for summers, it needed to be made fit for year-round living. Before 1942, Marguerite Shaughnessy had stayed for several winters in one of the apartments in the building next to the Shaughnessy coach house and stables on Montague Street (later the St. Andrews Dairy).

She was a very vital person, full of executive ability and energy, in her day a fine tennis player (with a vicious underhand serve), and an excellent left-handed golfer. During the Second World War she did many things. In Montreal she was chairman of "Wings for Britain" — a volunteer organization set up by Mr. J.W. McConnell, owner of the *Montreal Star*, to collect large sums of money to pay for Spitfires. She was also a senior official in the Canadian Red Cross.

In St. Andrews she and her sister Edith (Bud), the Hon. Mrs. Redmond, were instrumental in setting up the Mercury Club in 1942. Situated in the old *Homestead* building on Parr Street, this was a leave centre for men and women in the armed forces, primarily men of the R.A.F. Operational Station at Pennfield. Mr. and Mrs. Philip Green managed the Mercury Club, but Marguerite Shaughnessy was definitely the "Boss Lady" and gathered together a great number of volunteers, young and old, to assist her. The club was much needed in St. Andrews. The servicemen and servicewomen would stay for their forty-eight-hour leaves, and there was always some entertainment planned.

Fort Tipperary, built in 1902 on the site of the original Fort, which housed the British garrison in the War of 1812.
Private Collection

Several of the R.A.F. men married St. Andrews girls, and two of them, John Hull and Fynes Charlton, returned to the town to live and work for the rest of their lives, while others took their wives to other parts of Canada.

Marguerite Shaughnessy took a prominent part in the community before, during, and after the War. She even ran once for Council but was defeated. Perhaps it was just as well — such a forceful character might have taken over the whole town. Like all her family, Marg Shaughnessy, as she was known to friends, was not a bit stuck-up, and was generous and kind. Her Sealyham dogs would give visitors a noisy welcome at *The Fort*, with much tail wagging.

All the important visitors were still received at *The Fort* during Marguerite Shaughnessy's ownership. Prime Minister Mackenzie King stayed there, as did the Governor General, the Earl of Athlone, and his wife Princess Alice. Sometimes the Fort was let — and Lord Beaverbrook and a group of rather high-living friends had it for a few weeks one summer. Their Excellencies the Governor General Lord Alexander and Lady Alexander also rented it for a month in 1950 or 1951 with their family.

There was a tame seagull at *The Fort*, which sat on top of the flagpole and was fed a bowl of porridge every morning. When Lord Alexander rented the house, his personal standard was flown from the flagpole, whereupon the seagull — whose name was Sebastian — abandoned

The Hon. Marguerite Shaughnessy (left) and the Hon. Edith Mary Shaughnessy.

it and flew off to the *Algonquin*, where the Canadian flag (then the Red Ensign) was flying. He stayed there for the whole of the Alexanders' visit. Since he was a Shaughnessy seagull, perhaps he was just demonstrating that he was not a snob.

The Hon. Marguerite Shaughnessy died in St. Andrews on May 15, 1958, at the age of sixty-seven. She suffered a stroke a few years before she died, lost her speech, and was confined to a wheelchair. However, she still enjoyed seeing visitors, and children liked to call on her and never seemed intimidated by her inability to speak.

Marguerite's sister, the Hon. Mrs. Redmond, her husband René Redmond, and their only child, Margot, used to stay at the *Algonquin* during the summers of the late twenties and early thirties. They then rented *Glengarry*, Mrs. Farmer's house on Reed Avenue, from about 1933 to 1938, making a lovely garden at the rear. In 1938, René Redmond bought a farm at Bayside and called it *Bantry Bay*, and Herbie Raye became farm manager. A year later the Redmonds bought the McColl house on King Street.

In the First World War, René Redmond had a distinguished military career, being awarded the D.S.O and Bar for gallantry. Returning to civilian life, he went into the insurance business in Montreal. During the Second World War, the Redmonds contributed to the war effort in many ways. They were responsible for bringing Frau Dolfuss (the widow of the assassinated Chancellor of Austria) and her two children, a boy and a girl, to stay in St. Andrews. The Redmonds rented *Ifield Cottage* for the Dolfuss family. Rudi Dolfuss later attended Loyola College in Montreal.

In 1942 Bud Redmond donated a mobile canteen to the C.V.C. at St. Andrews. It was built in town and was an exact replica of those in use in Britain. Completely equipped with stoves, china, cutlery, etc., it could feed several hundred people and carry two stretchers. Bud Redmond also assisted her sister, Marguerite Shaughnessy, in establishing the Mercury Club.

Margot Redmond was in Montreal when war was declared, and joined the Canadian Red Cross in January 1940, becoming one of their most efficient ambulance drivers. Her unit was sent to Britain in 1943, and after a short time on the outskirts of London, they were posted to Italy. En route, their troop-ship was torpedoed. But Margot Redmond was fortunate to find a lifeboat with others from the ship and was rescued later.

After working in a British hospital in North Africa for a time, the Canadian Red Cross unit finally reached the Canadian troops fighting in Italy. Since women ambulance drivers were not allowed up to the front lines, the unit worked in the hospitals caring for the wounded when they arrived. They returned to Britain later with plans to go on to France, when fortunately the war ended. Margot Redmond returned to Canada on a hospital ship in June 1945. Three years later, on January 24, 1948, she married Norman Talbot Mais.

It was in 1948-1949 that René Redmond started the St. Andrews Dairy. The former Shaughnessy coach house and stables had been converted into a modern dairy and for the first time St. Andrews people had pasteurized milk — and though it is hard to believe now, there was some opposition to this at the time. Sydney Lord was one of the first to work at the dairy: before that, he would deliver "raw" milk from Earl Thomas while Mr. Redmond's dairyman would deliver milk from Bantry Bay Farm, with its prize herd of Jersey cows.

René Redmond was a handsome man with great charm

Howard W. Pillow (left) and René Redmond at the Old Men's Club, St. Andrews. Private Collection

and there was much sadness throughout St. Andrews when he died on July 21, 1955, at the age of sixty-six. His wife Bud continued to live in their house on King Street until 1959, when she moved to *Fort Tipperary* following her sister's death. She lived at *The Fort* until her death on December 13, 1964. Though Mrs. Redmond lived alone for those years, she was fortunate to have her daughter Margot, Norman, and their children living just down the hill in *Malahide*.

This branch of the Shaughnessy family came to St. Andrews in 1959, when Norman and Margot (Redmond) Mais bought their house on De Monts Road and moved permanently to the town with their four children: Peter, Susan, Mary (Terry), and Anthony (Tony). They called the house *Malahide* and lived there for five years. At the end of the road, it was private and quiet — a good home for children, to say nothing of the golden retrievers Margot Mais, a great animal lover, was breeding. There were always plenty of them about.

However, with the death of her mother, the Hon. Mrs. Redmond, *Fort Tipperary* was vacant again, and the Mais family was faced with a decision. The house was of historic importance, with great significance for the Shaughnessy family as well as for St. Andrews as a whole. The grandsons of Lord Shaughnessy — Thomas Shaughnessy, Alfred Shaughnessy, and the third

Lord Shaughnessy (William Graham) — were unable to live at *The Fort* because of either the cost or the inconvenience. And while there were other granddaughters besides Margot Mais, she was the only one who could take on the traditional St. Andrews home, though it was still a very big decision for a family with children. Living at *The Fort* was rather like living in a goldfish bowl. Next door to the *Algonquin*, it drew tourists and sightseers who were sometimes not reluctant to walk in and stare.

But Norman and Margot Mais also carried on the Shaughnessys' traditional hospitality, making *The Fort* available for Canadian Club, House and Garden visits, for Girl Guide and Curling Club annual dinners — and there was always a great deal of coming and going of family and young people. Margot Mais was by this time breeding Dandie Dinmonts, and though they had a large kennel, they were much in evidence. Norman Mais served on the town council and was chairman of the St. Andrews Library for many years.

Norman Mais died after a long illness in 1983. With her family grown up and some married, Margot Mais decided to leave *Fort Tipperary*, and it was sold to the Province of New Brunswick in 1985, thus ending eighty-three years of occupancy by the Shaughnessy family. In that year Margot Mais also built a house at Bantry Bay Farm, where she had always really wished to live. While the farm no longer had the prize Jersey herd for which it was renowned, it still teemed with life. There you could find donkeys, ponies, chickens, and, of course, the Mais dogs. Grandchildren live next door and others came to St. Andrews in the summer — another fifth generation family, now much more than merely "summer people." Margot Redmond Mais died in July 2004, at *Bantry Bay*, the place she loved the most. *Fort Tipperary* suffered serious fire damage that same year but was later reconstructed by the Province of New Brunswick.

The Hon. Ann Shaughnessy

51

Innisfree
Fiander Road, Bocabec

The Hon. Ann Shaughnessy was the youngest daughter of the second Lord and Lady Shaughnessy. She had spent all her childhood summers in St. Andrews, since her parents rented Number 5 Cottage at the *Algonquin* for about twenty-five years, travelling down from Montreal in the *Killarney*, the C.P.R. company railway car, and staying for two months. The children consisted of Peggy, Hazel (Bob), Ann, and an only son, William (Bill). Hazel was the only daughter to marry — her husband being James Ballantyne. They owned a house in St. Andrews, on Carleton Street (later the Donald McLeese house). James Ballantyne was the brother of Charles Ballantyne, who lived in St. Andrews.

Ann Shaughnessy bought a small house from Arthur Rogers at the far end of the Finander Road. It was built high on the rocks on the edge of the sea, overlooking Passamaquoddy Bay, and though it required a good deal of reconstruction, Ann Shaughnessy moved in sometime in the late 1950s and came down from Toronto every summer thereafter. She had a special love for both St. Andrews and Bocabec, and seemed to possess total recall of her summers by the sea. Her house was called *Innisfree*, after the "lake isle" in Yeats' poem, a place of peace and tranquility.

On her death in 1980, she left *Innisfree* to her brother, Lord William Graham Shaughnessy, the third Baron. He and his wife, who lived in London, England, during the rest of the year, came to Bocabec each summer. Bill Shaughnessy, who was born in 1922, inherited the title at the age of sixteen, on his father's death in 1938. In the Second World War he served overseas with the Canadian Grenadier Guards, holding the rank of Major. He married Mary Whitely, from Letchworth, England, in 1944.

Bill Shaughnessy and his family lived in Canada after the war, first in Montreal and later in Calgary. He had many business connections in the country but in time returned to Britain. He was a working member of the peerage, taking his seat in the House of Lords, and was often consulted on matters relating to the Commonwealth, particularly Canada. Friendly and ebullient, he not only represented his country overseas but was known as a good friend of St. Andrews — and one of our own people.

The Shaughnessys had two daughters, Kate and Bridget, and two sons. Their first-born son, Patrick, died young; his brother Michael became the fourth Baron Shaughnessy when their father died in 2003.

William Hope

Mr. and Mrs. William Hope built their house — which they called *Dalmeny* — in 1901, next door to the Maxwell house on the Bar Road, just above the railway tracks. Edward Maxwell, a close friend, was the architect. The house had spacious verandahs and a lovely garden. William Hope was a skilled artist, who later became a member of the Royal Canadian Academy of Arts (R.C.A.), and Edward Maxwell designed a delightful small studio for his use. The studio was saved when *Dalmeny* was destroyed by fire on June 10, 1946. Alas, it has fallen apart bit by bit since then. This large property is still owned by the Hope family.

William Hope's father was John Hope. He was originally from England and in the distilling business. He and his wife were among the earliest guests at the *Algonquin Hotel*, coming first in 1892, bringing their son William with them. William's wife was Constance Jarvis of Toronto, who came from a large, wealthy family. This was probably a good thing, since Willie Hope never really worked at anything except his painting.

In St. Andrews he often painted with G. Horne Russell and Sir William Van Horne. His studio was a meeting place for "gentleman artists" — where, as his daughter-in-law, Thea Hope, used to recall, no lady artists were invited. Willie Hope was also known for his manner of dress — sometimes wearing a long black cape and black hat, ruffles at the neck, beautiful silk ties and cravats — always immaculate in appearance. The famous Montreal painter Alphonse Jongers painted William Hope, and it is considered one of his finest portraits.

Mrs. William Hope was a forceful lady with a rather loud voice. She drove a carriage in tandem (two horses, one in front of the other) and would arrive with a great flourish at O'Neill's grocery store, call for someone to come out and take her order, then ride off back through town and out to the Bar Road again. The Hopes had two children: John Charles and Constance. John Charles Hope married Dorothea (Thea) Pitcairn Cockburn, daughter of Francis Jeffery Cockburn. Mr. Cockburn was with the Bank of Montreal (he later became

Dalmeny, the home of William Hope, designed by Edward Maxwell.

D. Will McKay

general manager) in Quebec City, Mexico, and later Montreal. Constance (Connie) Hope married Wayne Davidson, and they had one daughter, Hope, who married Michael Dibben.

Charles Hope and his wife Thea built a house during the 1920s, on land just opposite his parents' home on the Bar Road. They had four sons: John Charles William (Bill), Frank, Robert, and Peter. The eldest, Bill, joined the R.C.A.F. in the Second World War and was killed in action — a tragic loss to the family. Charles and Thea Hope lived in Montreal, where he had a small printing business, but they came to St. Andrews every summer and their Bar Road house was a busy place, with young people always coming and going.

The Hopes were also very fond of sailing. Charles' father, William, had chartered the yacht *Barracuda*, whose sailing master was Capt. Robert Maloney. This vessel had been owned previously by Franklin Roosevelt and was later purchased by the Hopes, who would take out parties of friends, sometimes for all-day affairs with a picnic lunch at Pendleton Beach or elsewhere. The yacht was sold in 1946 to Herman Bartlett. He had been in the R.C.A.F. during the Second World War and used his demobilisation gratuity to buy the *Barracuda*, which had been lying on its keel on Navy Island for ten years and was consequently offered at a bargain price.

Their son Robert Hope sold the Bar Road house to Mr. and Mrs. D.G. Rouse, of Fredericton in 1975. The Charles Hopes had moved in 1962 to Prince of Wales Street, almost opposite *Fort Tipperary*. Their new residence was a converted coach house moved from the Macklem-Walsh property beside the arena. Enlarged, it made a charming house, with a delightful small garden at the back. The Hopes had ten good years in their new house. There were fewer responsibilities and fortunately no money worries. As their friends observed, they kept receiving goodly amounts from various estates on both sides of the family. For instance, Mrs. George Hooper, of Montreal, was an aunt of Charles Hope. It was she who gave Greenock Church its Manse in 1900, and paid for the distinguished architect Edward Maxwell to design it. When she died, Charles Hope was one of her heirs.

Thea Hope was a fine and talented person. There seemed to be nothing she could not do. She was an expert needlewoman, cook, gardener, house painter, and carpenter, when necessary. She was also well read and an exceptionally good amateur artist. Yet she never spoke about her own accomplishments. She continued to come to St. Andrews for ten years after her husband died in 1972 at the age of seventy-four. Thea Hope was always so active she never seemed to grow old. The small white Volkswagen she owned could be seen all over the place: at the Bar Road, where she knew a secret place to pick lilies-of-the-valley; at Harding's Point, where she picked pints of wild strawberries; at some obscure beach, where she and her friends would swim in the cold salt water — or on a quick dash upriver. She never appeared to rest but at the same time was a wonderfully restful person to be with.

Dorothea Pitcairn Hope died on April 23, 1983. She was eighty-two years old.

7

Kingsbrae, 1898

Torn down, 1971

Top of King Street

Donald McMaster and H.W. Pillow

Donald McMaster, a prominent Montreal lawyer and later a member of the British House of Commons, built his large house at the top of King Street in 1898 — one year after his neighbour, T.R. Wheelock, had built his.

In the early 1920s *Kingsbrae* was purchased by Mr. and Mrs. Percy Cowans, also from Montreal. Percy Cowans was a senior stockbroker with the firm of McDougall & Cowans, and he and his wife spent summers in St. Andrews with their family until 1931. They had five children — Anna, Ruth, Fred, Percy, and John. Anna and Ruth were great riders whose saddle horses were brought down from Montreal by train and stabled in a barn at the corner of Parr and Adolphus streets.

Unfortunately, Mr. and Mrs. Cowans had to sell *Kingsbrae* in 1931. John, the youngest child, was only a boy then, but in 1971 he returned to St. Andrews to take up permanent resi-

Howard W. Pillow's boat, the Lucinda.

Private Collection

dence. He and his wife Betty had been living in Montreal, and they bought the former David R. Forgan house on Carleton Street. Their son Fred married Edward Maxwell's granddaughter, Lee Woodd-Cahusac — a bond with the early days of St. Andrews as a resort.

In 1932, Mr. and Mrs. Howard Winthrop Pillow, of Montreal bought *Kingsbrae.* Howard Pillow was born in Montreal in 1883; his wife Lucile (née Fairbanks) was American. They were no strangers to St. Andrews, as they had often stayed at the *Algonquin Hotel,* and Howard Pillow's father, Sam Pillow, was half-brother to Mrs. Charles Hosmer. It was the Hosmer connection which first brought the Pillows to St. Andrews.

Howard Pillow was President of the British American Bank Note Company, and he was well liked both in his business circles and locally in St. Andrews, where he was an active member of the Old Men's Club. Local friends liked him for not putting on airs and for being genuinely interested in what they were doing. A rather large, strong man, he had the most charming smile and was easy with all ages.

Kingsbrae, built in 1898. Private Collection

The Pillows enjoyed people and liked to entertain. It was a great sight to see their fifty-six-foot cabin cruiser, the *Lucinda I* and later the *Lucinda II,* leave the town wharf every day at two p.m. for an outing in the bay with the Pillow family and guests. Capt. Cliff Brown was skipper, and was succeeded on his retirement by Capt. Arthur Sirles. The *Lucinda II* was later owned by Murray Vaughan, who married the Pillows' only child, Marguerite.

Howard Pillow died in 1952, at the age of sixty-nine. Lucile Pillow died in 1969. After their deaths, it was decided to tear down *Kingsbrae* — a hard and sad decision.

Sir Charles Tupper

In 1872 Dr. Charles and Mrs. Tupper bought land, including a stone house, from Joseph Walton. It was situated about four miles from St. Andrews on the Saint John Road. The house had been built by Capt. Robert D. James some time after 1844, when he first came to New Brunswick. The Tuppers called it *Highland Hill*.

Best known as one of the Fathers of Confederation, Sir Charles Tupper was born in Amherst, Nova Scotia, in 1821, and later studied medicine at Edinburgh University. He continued to practice as a physician after he entered politics and had a seat in the House of Commons. He was knighted in 1879, and in 1883 he was appointed High Commissioner to London, where he remained for thirteen enjoyable years, before being recalled to Ottawa to become Prime Minister in 1896 for a six-month term. After his retirement from public life, Sir Charles went to live in Britain where he was made a baronet in 1888. He died at his home in Kent in 1915.

Sir Charles' political life kept him away from St. Andrews for much of the time, but Mrs. Tupper and their six children, three sons and three daughters, came frequently and loved it. There is an account of Emma, one of the girls, "riding to her heart's content." Dr. Tupper had the reputation of being a very fashionable doctor and had many lady patients. Fanny Meredith, wife of Edmund Meredith, of Ottawa, was one favourite. The families were close friends and the Merediths came to St. Andrews with the Tuppers in 1873, a long and difficult journey from Ottawa. Since *Highland Hill* was a small house, Fanny boarded in St. Andrews with her children. Next year the Merediths stayed with the Tuppers, since Fanny was seven months pregnant when she arrived. She gave birth to her son, Coly, at *Highland Hill*. Coly Meredith became a well-known architect in later life.

Because St. Andrews was then so difficult to reach and the Tuppers were so often away, *Highland Hill* was frequently let. In 1878 it was rented by Alex Gilmour, and at that time there was a fire that did much damage to the interior. The house was eventually sold to Nathan Blakeney, a nephew of the Tuppers, and later to Senator Robert Mackay.

Opposite: Highland Hill, the original house of Sir Charles Tupper. Private Collection

Sir Thomas Tait

The plans for *Linkscrest* were drawn sometime between 1918 and 1924, but the house was not built until 1928-1929. It was an imposing red brick house in the Georgian style, quite different from Maxwell's other St. Andrews houses. Situated on the edge of the original golf course, near the 13th tee, it had a magnificent view of St. Andrews Harbour.

Sir Thomas and Lady Tait stayed at the *Algonquin* for several years before they built their house. Their daughter, Mrs. Winnifred Fourney, was confined to a wheelchair, and perhaps this was the reason why the Taits did not build for almost ten years after they received the first plans. Scientists who worked at the Biological Station at that time and passed by the *Linkscrest* site each day remembered that Sir Thomas had a great deal of the landscaping done before building. There were the pond, lawns, and flower gardens, and later a tennis court was laid.

Born in Melbourne, Canada East (modern Quebec) in 1864, Sir Thomas Tait was the son of Sir Melbourne Tait. He was Private Secretary to Sir William Van Horne between 1882 and 1886 and later became general manager of transportation for the C.P.R. In 1903 the Australian government appointed him chairman of the Board of Railway Commissioners for Victoria. After seven years in Australia, he returned to Canada in 1910. It was for this service that he was knighted in 1911. He retired to private life in 1916.

Sir Thomas was a genial man with a rather large florid face. He was fond of sailing and owned the *Pakwan*, formerly T.R. Wheelock's yacht. There was no yacht club house at that time — indeed, there was no yacht club. But Sir Thomas appointed himself "commodore" anyway, almost always wearing a white yachting cap. He liked to be at the end of the wharf when the large American yachts, like the Vanderbilts' and the Atwater Kents', came in. Much to the amusement of local fishermen, he would greet the visitors as commodore of the non-existent St. Andrews yacht club. Sir Thomas died at *Linkscrest* on July 25, 1940, at the age of seventy-six.

Lady Tait was large and kindly, delightful to all her guests. The Taits gave wonderful old-fashioned tennis parties during the 1930s, with everyone in their whites, and delicious afternoon teas.

During the Second World War, *Linkscrest* was used as a convalescent home for R.A.F. and R.C.A.F. personnel. There were thirty-five beds and an air force staff of thirty. When the war ended, *Linkscrest* stood empty for a couple of years, but in 1947 it was purchased by Dr. Gavin Miller, a noted Montreal surgeon, and Mrs. Miller. To the Tait property of twenty-five acres, the Millers added another twenty-five when they bought an adjacent property from Dr. H.P. O'Neill.

Kitty Miller was a notable gardener and thus the Tait estate was restored to its former beauty. After Dr. Miller's death, *Linkscrest* was bought by Dr. John Riddell, the Managing Director of Mount Pleasant Mines, and Mrs. Riddell. It was later sold to the Huntsman Marine Science Centre, renamed *Anderson House* after Dr. John Anderson, and used as a residence for students and visitors to the Centre.

The Linkscrest, owned by Sir Thomas Tait, designed by Edward Maxwell. Private Collection

Col. Frank Hume and
Mr. and Mrs. Douglas Ambridge

Col. Frank Hume, from Houlton, Maine, built his summer cottage at Brandy Cove in 1908, far away from other summer cottages, on the shore of the St. Croix River looking across to Maine. Soon after the outbreak of the First World War, Col. Hume decided to sell, and in 1916 *Brandy Cove* was purchased by Mr. Fred P. McNichol of St. Stephen. His son, Frank McNichol, was the next owner. Mr. and Mrs. A.W. Guinness (Tony and Diana) then purchased the house sometime in the early 1950s, and later sold it to Mr. and Mrs. Douglas Ambridge from Toronto.

Douglas Ambridge was the President of Abitibi Pulp & Paper. Jessie Ambridge was musical, artistic, and a gifted gardener. They had four daughters, two of whom were married — so there were grandchildren to enjoy the garden and beach. Many wonderful parties for all ages were given by the Ambridges.

Up the hill from the garden, where the Huntsman Marine Science Centre nature walk now winds its way, Doug Ambridge had a spring of pure water walled in, with wooden seats around it. Here he would gather his cronies to sit and sip the whisky that tasted so much better with the crystalline water — and share equally sparkling conversation.

In the early 1970s, he sold the house and all his country estate to the federal government, which let it to what was then the Huntsman Marine Laboratory. Since *Brandy Cove* was next door to the Department of Fisheries and Oceans Biological Station, the location was ideal.

Col. Frank Hume's cottage, later owned by
Mr. and Mrs. Douglas Ambridge.

Private Collection

Robert S. Gardiner

16
Hillside, 1893
Renamed *Gillcairn*, 1911
De Monts Road

The house Robert Gardiner built in St. Andrews was the first summer cottage in the town (followed by the Inness cottage a few months later). Robert Gardiner and his wife had been summer visitors since 1879; when the *Argyll Hotel* was built in 1881, they were among the first guests, and after 1889 the Gardiners stayed at the *Algonquin* each summer until their own cottage was built.

Robert Gardiner was President of the Rand Avery Supply Company of Boston. As Vice-President of the St. Andrews Land Company, which built the *Algonquin* in addition to other projects, he became very influential in promoting St. Andrews as a resort. Robert Gardiner was responsible for getting the golf course started and personally donated the clubhouse. In its early days, Rand Avery Supply Company printed railway tickets and menus. It was through this connection that Robert Gardiner got to know Sir William Van Horne. It has always been claimed that, in turn, it was Robert Gardiner who first interested Sir William in St. Andrews as a summer retreat.

Robert Gardiner was also an extensive traveller, having made a round-the-world trip and visited China and Japan a number of times. He later wrote a book about Japan and lectured on both countries. His daughter, Alice, also a remarkable person, married William T. Payne, an American who later represented C.P.R. Steamships in Japan, where he and his wife lived in Yokohama. William Payne became general manager of C.P.R. Steamships for both Japan and China, retiring in 1922 after residing in Japan for forty-three years. Mr. and Mrs. Payne then lived in New York. After her father's death, Mrs. Payne spent the summers in St. Andrews at *Hillside* until it was sold in 1911 to Mr. and Mrs. Robert Gill of Ottawa.

The Gills, with their sons Henry, Evan, and Francis, loved the house and renamed it *Gillcairn*. Edward Maxwell drew up plans for additions and alterations carried out in 1915. The Gills' sons continued to summer at *Gillcairn* with their wives and families until it was sold in 1956 to Gen. and Mrs. James A. Van Fleet.

Opposite: Robert S. Gardiner's cottage, built in 1893 and later known as Gillcairn.
D. Will McKay

Robert S. Gardiner, builder of the first summer cottage in St. Andrews (1893).

Private Collection

During the time that Mrs. Van Fleet was making some major changes at *Gillcairn*, the General had bought the Curtis Wells house at Dominion Hill outside St. Andrews, where he and his family and guests stayed until 1960, when *Gillcairn* was ready. Cyrus Curtis, of the Curtis Publishing Company (*Saturday Evening Post*, etc.), had built the house at Dominion Hill for his daughter, on 125 acres of land. One night, at a dinner party in New York, Mrs. Van Fleet, a very pretty and charming woman, was complaining about the heat and humidity of summers in Florida, where she and her husband lived. One of the Curtises then said, "We have a house for sale in St. Andrews, New Brunswick, and the air is heavenly there." The Van Fleets replied, "We'll buy it" — and they did.

Gen. James Alward Van Fleet, from Hobe Sound, Florida, was physically a giant of a man, and also a great American soldier. During the Second World War and afterwards he served in Europe. In 1947, he became the Deputy Chief of Staff of the European Command and was stationed at Frankfurt. During the Korean War, from 1951 to 1953, he commanded the United Nations forces. He was still active at the age of ninety-eight, though his health was failing, and he lived to see his hundredth birthday in 1992. Mrs. Van Fleet, who loved *Gillcairn* and St. Andrews, died some years before her husband.

Ownership of *Gillcairn* passed to the Van Fleet's daughter, Dempsie Catherine, and her husband, Maj. Gen. J.A. McChristian of Hobe Sound, Florida. Their home welcomed family and guests for over a century.

Jeremiah Smith Jr.

Judge Jeremiah Smith, of Boston, came to St. Andrews at the turn of the century to stay at the *Algonquin Hotel* with his daughter, Miss Elizabeth H. Smith (Beth), and his son, Jeremiah Smith Jr. (Jerry). Soon afterwards, Jeremiah Smith Jr. bought land from Mrs. G.M. Bosworth on what is now Acadia Road. He built a house on this site in October 1915 — for which Mr. John W. Ames of Cambridge, Massachusetts, was the architect.

Judge Smith was a Professor of Law at the Harvard Law School, and he and his children spent several happy summers in St. Andrews until his death there in 1921. After his death, his son and daughter continued to summer at their St. Andrews house for many years.

They were energetic people. The judge rode every day, hiring his horse from Mr. Mallory's livery stable. Miss Beth was an enthusiastic golfer, playing daily, and she is remembered playing to an advanced age. She was indeed a memorable figure: with snow-white hair, walking with a determined stride. In her last years, however, she became very frail. But she still came to St. Andrews from Cambridge, Massachusetts, in an ambulance. She died in 1956.

Mr. Jeremiah Smith Jr., an outstanding lawyer and banker, was a member of the Boston law firm Herrick, Smith, Donald & Farley. During his St. Andrews summers he played golf and tennis and sailed his own boat. Nevertheless, his visits had to be fitted in between the demands of his legal career and service abroad. After the First World War he worked for the Rockefeller War Relief Commission in Rumania, Belgium, and Turkey. Later he served in Paris as the United States member of the Financial Committee of the Peace Conference, conferring at different times with Lloyd George, Clemenceau, and Woodrow Wilson.

In 1924 he began his most challenging job, having been appointed the League of Nations' Commissioner General for Hungary. His task was to remake the financial structure of the country — and he completed his work in two years rather than the five which had been allotted. At the end of his term he refused his salary, and when the Hungarian people offered him £100,000, he declined that too, with thanks. Instead, he asked that a Jeremiah Smith Jr. Scholarship be set up for Hungarian technical students to be trained in the United States.

Jeremiah Smith Jr. died on March 12, 1935, at the age of sixty-four. At his death an editorial in the *New York Times* on March 14th declared that "the last of the four who have borne the name has given it a wider acquaintance and fame. There was not a country in the civilized world that did not know of the extraordinary achievements of Jeremiah Smith, Jr., in saving the financial life of Hungary in her time of crisis." He and his remarkable family are still remembered in St. Andrews with affection and admiration.

In October 1959, after Miss Beth Smith's death, the Acadia Road house was sold to Mr. and Mrs. Louis Kronenberger. They made one major change in the exterior by removing the upstairs porch that Miss Smith had added in the 1920s, thus returning the house to Jack Ames' original design.

Emmy Plaut Kronenberger knew St. Andrews well, having come in 1915 as a child and for many summers afterwards. Louis Kronenberger enjoyed their summers here and came almost every year until his death in 1980. He was a scholar of great distinction, a brilliant student, and teacher of English language and literature. He had been a visiting lecturer at Oxford, Harvard, and other universities; drama critic for *Time* magazine from 1938 to 1961; literary editor at Alfred Knopf; and a novelist. As owner of the house on Acadia Road, he was a worthy successor to the Jeremiah Smiths.

T.R. Wheelock and Florence Ayscough

8

Original house, 1897
Named *Topside*, c. 1930
Top of King Street

Mr. Thomas Wheelock was a native of Nova Scotia. He and his wife had lived for many years in Shanghai, China, where he was a merchant on a large scale, owning a fleet of cargo boats which went to the mouth of the Yangtze to load and unload the big foreign ships. They first visited St. Andrews in 1881, bringing a few Chinese servants with them and staying at the *Argyll Hotel*, which had just opened. In 1889, after Mr. Wheelock had retired and they were living in Boston, they returned to St. Andrews and the *Argyll*. It was then that they took a great liking to the large McRoberts property, purchasing it for $3,000 from David McRoberts. Although there were plans for building a new house and a site was staked out, the scheme foundered and the property was conveyed back to David McRoberts in 1893. During this time, however, the Wheelocks used to picnic on the land and had a bathhouse built down near the shore on the shipyard lot. They drove out in their carriage along the well-built road they had installed at considerable cost (later the paved driveway to *Strathcroix*, the home of David and Willa Walker, who bought the McRoberts property in 1953).

In 1897, however, the Wheelocks built a large and very fine house at the top of King Street — the builder being David McRoberts. On the death of her parents, the Wheelocks' daughter, Florence Wheelock Ayscough, inherited their St. Andrews house. She had married Francis Ayscough, an Englishman, in 1888. They also lived in Shanghai, where she became an international authority on the customs and traditions of the Chinese people. The author of many books, she also collaborated with the poet Amy Lowell in publishing translations of Chinese poetry. Living in Germany, later, Florence Wheelock learned German in order to translate books on China written in that language.

She loved her many little Pekinese dogs and wrote several books about one in particular, named Yo Fu. Miss Lucille Douglas, a friend and artist, did the illustrations for *Firecracker Land*, one of Florence Ayscough's best-known books, and visited her in St. Andrews. When Mrs. Ayscough donated the tea room operated by the I.O.D.E., Lucille Douglas did the

133

murals. (This small log building near the Block House was later owned by the Town of St. Andrews.)

The Ayscoughs also owned a charming log cabin on McMaster Island (sometimes familiarly called Mac or Ayscough Island), near Deer Island. Mrs. Ayscough loved to entertain her guests for lunch there and many friends would sail over to visit. Capt. Martin Brown was master of the Ayscoughs' yacht, the *Yu Yuin*, while Capt. John Calder was in charge of their motor launch, the *Irish Rose*. Capt. Calder's wife and their son, Emerson, worked for Mrs. Ayscough and used to take care of the island and its cabin. They retained many fond memories of those years.

In June 1927, Governor General Lord Willingdon and Lady Willingdon were visiting St. Andrews, and Mrs. Ayscough entertained them on Mac Island, also arranging a gathering there of all the fishing boats and their owners. Unfortunately, it was a very foggy day. However, a

Topside, built in 1897. Private Collection

134

group photograph was taken on the shore of all the visitors. At the centre of a great crowd are Lord Willingdon with dark overcoat and bowler hat, his wife with large hat and pearls, and Mrs. Ayscough also smartly hatted.

Mr. and Mrs. Ayscough went to live on Guernsey in the Channel Islands, and that is where Francis Ayscough died. Two years later, Florence Ayscough married Prof. Harley Farnsworth MacNair of the University of Chicago, also an expert on China. Married in Guernsey, they went to Chicago to live. Florence Wheelock Ayscough MacNair died in 1942, and in her will she left the Charlotte County Historical Society a generous gift of Chinese porcelain screens, tables, jade vases, and other artifacts, which had been in her St. Andrews house. These are now part of the collection of the Charlotte County Museum in St. Stephen.

The Wheelock-Ayscough house was bought in the 1930s by Mr. and Mrs. Robert Struthers of Norton, Connecticut, and named *Topside*. Mr. Struthers was physically a very large man and known as Uncle Bob to his younger friends. He was a Wall Street broker and owned a yacht called *Belinda*, of which Capt. Martin Brown, who had been with the Ayscoughs, was the master. Mr. and Mrs. Struthers and their friends spent every fine day cruising in Passamaquoddy Bay. Mrs. Struthers died in 1968, about ten years after her husband, at the age of ninety.

Topside was then bought by A. Murray Vaughan and later by James Oppe and his wife, Mona, who moved to St. Andrews from Montreal in 1970.

Florence Ayscough (left) with Governor General Lord Willingdon and Lady Willingdon at a reception for fishermen held on McMaster Island, June 17, 1927.

Private Collection

Opposite: The G. Horne Russell house, designed by Maxwell & Pitts (1924). E.H. Snell

G. Horne Russell

Built in 1924 by Mr. and Mrs. Horne Russell, and designed by Maxwell & Pitts, *Derry Bay* is a lovely stucco house with a studio at one end, with a fine large window to provide a north light. Situated on the waterfront on Joe's Point Road, the house has a fine view of St. Andrews Harbour.

G. Horne Russell was born in Banff, Scotland, in 1861. Showing great artistic talent from an early age, he studied art in Edinburgh and London, and developed a particular talent for portraiture. In 1889, at the age of twenty-eight, he was persuaded to move to Canada and "grow up with the country." In the same year, he married Elizabeth Morrison, of Banchory, Aberdeenshire.

He opened a studio in Montreal and before long acquired many clients — among them some of the most famous Canadians of the time: Sir Wilfred Laurier, Lord Strathcona, and Lord Shaughnessy were painted by him, among many others. Russell was very far from a sedentary artist, however, and was not content to wait for sitters to come to him. A tall, vigorous man, he loved the outdoors, especially the sea, and took every opportunity to explore this unknown country. Fortunately, the Grand Trunk Railway gave him a commission in 1909 to paint the Rockies, and after several months among the vast mountains of the west he returned to paint large and impressive canvases of what he had seen. These "portraits" of the Rockies were much more than a commission for Russell; they contained his vision of a majestic new land, and he looked upon this period as of the greatest importance to his development as a landscape artist.

The C.P.R. later employed Russell to design many posters for their hotels and ships and to illustrate brochures for their hotels. He even painted postcards, many of which are collectors' items today. This highly paid commercial work gave him the chance to travel — and when he returned to his Montreal studio the portrait commissions continued to flow in. His pictures are now publicly displayed in the National Gallery in Ottawa; the Art Gallery of Ontario in

G. Horne Russell at the railway station in St. Andrews. C.P.R.

Toronto; the Musée des Beaux-Arts in Montreal; and the Beaverbrook Gallery in Fredericton. G. Horne Russell was made an R.C.A. in 1919.

Once financially secure, he could afford a country house and chose St. Andrews because of his love of the sea and his many connections with the C.P.R. in the town. He and his wife, with their two children, came almost every summer. Their son Norman, also an artist, and daughter Elizabeth (later Mrs. A.J. Mackenzie) came to enjoy *Derry Bay* almost as much as their parents did.

After a brief illness at his home in St. Andrews, G. Horne Russell died on June 24, 1933, and was buried in the St. Andrews Rural Cemetery.

After her husband's death, Mrs. Russell continued to spend her summers at *Derry Bay*, while later Norman Russell inherited the house and also continued to visit for several years. He eventually sold the house to Mr. and Mrs. Brian Devlin, of Montreal, who had been summer visitors for many years, staying mainly at the *Roof Tree*, Miss Edith Cummings' popular guesthouse on Queen Street. The Devlins wished to retire to St. Andrews and live year-round. This meant that *Derry Bay* had to be winterized. But the only place for a furnace (since there was no basement) was G. Horne Russell's studio — and there, alas, it was installed. The house was sold again after Mr. and Mrs. Devlin died.

Later owners included Dr. and Mrs. Alfred Needler. Dr. Needler, O.B.E., C.M., a highly respected marine scientist, was a former Deputy Minister of Fisheries in Ottawa.

David R. Forgan

This house has a more varied history than its neighbours. Originally, it was a small house called the *Queen Anne Cottage*, or *Park Cottage*, built by the St. Andrews Land Company in 1888-1889 on the Eastern Commons (now Indian Point) as a show house of the type to be built on their proposed development there. It was moved to its present location soon afterwards and sometimes used as a guest cottage by the *Algonquin Hotel*. In 1900 it was bought by Mr. and Mrs. David Forgan, who lived at that time in Chicago.

David R. Forgan was a Scotsman who had come to Canada in 1879 to join the Bank of Nova Scotia head office in Halifax. His elder brother, James, was already an accountant there, and right-hand man to Thomas Fyshe, the brilliant manager of the head office. When David Forgan was moved to the branch office in Fredericton, New Brunswick, he and his family visited St. Andrews, where they stayed at the *Algonquin Hotel*. Perhaps it was because he was born in St. Andrews, Fife, that David Forgan was so impressed.

Mrs. Forgan (née Agnes Kerr) came from Winnipeg — where David Forgan had been sent as accountant to the branch there (the first venture by the Bank of Nova Scotia outside the Maritimes). For his journey out west, he was given $40,000 in cash, to be carried by him in a leather bag. The journey took several days, and he could not be parted from his trust for a second. Later, in his own *Sketches & Speeches*, he recounted what a burden this had been!

After a time both Forgan brothers moved to Chicago, where James became President of the First National Bank and David Vice-President, both men of wealth and substance. However, the David Forgan family never forgot St. Andrews and still owned *Queen Anne Cottage*. They enlarged it greatly, laying out a large garden and a tennis court. Each summer they travelled from Chicago to spend months at St. Andrews with their children. There were five: Robert (Bob), Marion, Ethel — all born in Fredericton, New Brunswick — David R. Jr., and Russell (born in Minneapolis and Chicago respectively).

David Forgan liked playing golf, talking about it, and even making speeches about the

Park Cottage, later part of the Forgan House. Private Collection

Forgan House. D. Will McKay

game to bankers and senior businessmen. He liked to recall how as a wee Scots laddie of five he had learned to play the game on the Old Course at St. Andrews, Scotland, playing with a small specially made club and using the recently introduced gutta percha balls which had supplanted the feather-filled leather ones. He played many a game on the St. Andrews (Canada) course and was one of the important personages for whom caddies really liked to caddy.

At the end of the summer, leaving St. Andrews was always a big occasion, when people went to the railway station to bid goodbye to friends and their children. If travellers had a drawing-room on the train, they could ask to have it made up ahead of time — and year after year Mrs. Forgan delighted two little girls by being there as they left, and also by secretly placing a large marshmallow under each of the pillows on their made-up bunks.

Marion Forgan married Halstead Freeman, and Ethel married Lyndon P. Dodge. Both families lived in New York City and both built summer houses in St. Andrews on Joe's Point

Road, to which they came every summer. Marion Forgan Freeman, in particular, did a great deal to help and support St. Andrews organizations. She took a special interest in Greenock Church; and having herself experienced an operation and treatment at the Charlotte County Hospital, she and her friends helped that institution at a time of acute financial need.

David Forgan Freeman and his wife Hazel later owned the former Halstead Freeman house. They were regular visitors to the town for many years, along with their five children and their families. David and Hazel Freeman's grandchildren represent the fifth generation of the family in St. Andrews.

Berwick Brae was let for several years and then bought by Mr. and Mrs. Jack MacFarlane, and later by Mr. and Mrs. George Durgan. In 1971 it was purchased by Mr. and Mrs. John C. Cowans of Montreal, who furnished it with lovely things brought by them from Montreal. John Cowans spent some of his childhood summers in St. Andrews; his father, Percy Cowans, owned *Kingsbrae*, the Donald McMaster house at the top of King Street, which was the summer home of Mr. and Mrs. Howard Pillow for many years.

Mr. and Mrs. David Forgan and family. Left to right: Robert; Mrs. Forgan; Marion; David Sr.; David Jr.; Russell; Ethel.

Private Collection

The Rev. Alexander Bowser and Charles T. Ballantyne

The Rev. and Mrs Alexander Bowser were living in Concord, Massachusetts, when they built their summer cottage in St. Andrews in 1898, situated on what is now *Cedar Lane*. The Bowsers owned a lot of land stretching right down to *Pottery Creek*, previously owned by the Carroll family who were related to Mrs. Alphonsus O'Neill. *Cedar Croft* was an impressive summer cottage with a coachhouse, stable, and large barn for hay. It was the fourth summer cottage built in St. Andrews.

Alexander Bowser was born in Sackville, New Brunswick, in 1848. He went to Boston as a young man and graduated from Harvard in 1877. At one time he and his wife lived in St. Louis, and when they came from there to St. Andrews for summers they brought their black servants. The Bowsers had several horses and carriages. They had two sons, Robert (Bobby) and Henry. Both were married and lived in Massachusetts but visited St. Andrews frequently with their wives — Bobby, in particular, had many golfing friends. Henry was in the investment business in Boston and prospered greatly.

The Bowsers and their children were Unitarians, and the Rev. Bowser sometimes preached in the Methodist church in St. Andrews. While much has been forgotten about their life in St. Andrews, one little item fixed itself in the memory of the town. Guests who were invited to lunch or dinner at the Bowsers, especially the irreverent young, were much amused by the Rev. Bowser's habit, when the main meal was served, of looking at his wife and saying, "Thank you, mother dear." The remark is still remembered — indeed, one family adopted it as their own and passed it on to two further generations with pleasure and amusement.

Mrs. Adelaide R. Bowser died in January 1933 and her husband two months later — both in Concord, Massachusetts.

Robert Bowser sold *Cedar Croft* to Charles T. Ballantyne, of Montreal, in 1944. Charlie Ballantyne was then a very well-known lawyer; his father was the Hon. Senator C.C. Ballantyne, and Charles and his brothers, James and Murray, had stayed as children with

Opposite: Cedar Croft, built by the Rev. A. Bowser in 1898. D. Will McKay

143

Bellenden, the home of Mr. and Mrs. Charles Ballantyne. John Cowans

their parents at the *Algonquin Hotel*. Charles had married Rosalie Brittain, from Winnipeg, and they made substantial alterations to the Bowser house, both internally and externally, converting it for year-round use. They also changed the name to *Bellenden*. A few years after these changes had been made, Mr. and Mrs. Ballantyne took up permanent residence in St. Andrews and Mrs. Ballantyne's mother, Mrs. Ethel (Charlotte) Brittain, came to live with them. Their daughter, Rosalie Ann (Mrs. James Patterson), and son, Charles Colquhoun (Tim), had spent their childhood summers in St. Andrews and brought their own families with them after they married.

Charlie Ballantyne retired from his law practice in Montreal in 1950 at the age of forty-eight. But both he and his wife Rosalie became very active citizens of St. Andrews and Charlotte County. During the eleven years he was chairman of the Charlotte County Hospital board, from 1954 to 1965, Charlie Ballantyne did a tremendous amount of work, especially in fundraising. Rosalie Ballantyne was a strong member of All Saints Church and was one of the first members from St. Andrews on the Charlotte County Hospital Auxiliary, for which she worked for over twenty-five years. She supported a variety of other good causes, including the St. Andrews Town Library, and was held in much esteem and affection for her great generosity.

The garden at *Bellenden* was one of the best in St. Andrews. The Ballantyne flowers seemed to grow taller and better than anywhere else. Some said it was the good farm soil from the Bowser days. But Rosalie Ballantyne was more than a knowledgeable gardener — she worked long and hard, and so did her mother, Charlotte Brittain, who insisted, even when she was quite elderly, on digging out every single dandelion on the lawns with her own special long trowel. Meanwhile, the former coachhouse at *Bellenden* was made into a small house to accommodate the Ballantynes' family when they visited from London, England, and Scarsdale, New York.

Charlie Ballantyne died in St. Andrews in 1966, Mrs. Brittain in 1971, and Rosalie Ballantyne in Bermuda in 1982. They are all buried in St. John the Baptist Anglican Chapel of the Ease Cemetery, Chamcook. Rosalie Ballantyne had found *Bellenden* too large for her after the deaths of her husband and mother and moved to the converted coachhouse, where she lived with her devoted friend and helpmeet, Mrs. Christie Hope. She later moved to Bermuda to avoid the winters. The coachhouse was by then owned by Christie Hope, who sold it to Mr. and Mrs. Rowland Frazee of Montreal in 1981, when Mr. Frazee was President of the Royal Bank of Canada. *Bellenden* had been sold six months earlier to Mr. and Mrs. Howard B. Hodgson, from Boston. They were familiar with St. Andrews because Bunny Hodgson (Muriel Peabody) was the daughter of Mr. and Mrs. Gorham Hubbard. Her parents had been long-time summer visitors, and permanent residents after they built their house on Edward Street near the Kirk.

Rosalie Ballantyne (Mrs. Charles Ballantyne). Private Collection

Senator Robert Mackay and the Wilson Family at Clibrig

49

Clibrig, 1905-1906
Clibrig II, 1973
Saint John Road

In 1905, Senator and Mrs. Robert Mackay, of Montreal, bought 320 acres of beautiful farmland from Nathan Blakeney, a nephew of Sir Charles Tupper. Senator Mackay also bought Sir Charles Tupper's old stone house and other land, including shorefront property at Chamcook Harbour. The Tupper house, *Highland Hill*, needed much renovation, and Senator Mackay added a garage with an apartment above, built of stone like the original house. The large and spacious new house, designed by Finley & Spence of Montreal, was built on high ground with a magnificent view of Minister's Island and the bay beyond. The Mackays called their house *Clibrig*.

Robert Mackay, born in Caithness, Scotland, in 1840, emigrated to Montreal at the age of fifteen. After studying bookkeeping, he joined his uncles' dry goods business. Joseph and Edward Mackay, bachelor brothers from Sutherlandshire in Scotland, had made millions in this business, and when they died the estate went to their nephew Robert. In 1871, he married Jane, daughter of George Baptist of Trois-Rivières, Quebec — one of the province's Scottish lumber barons. Robert Mackay retired from the dry-goods business in 1893 and expanded his interests to some thirty prosperous companies, becoming one of the most prominent financiers in Canada — a director of sixteen companies, of which the C.P.R. and the Bank of Montreal were the most important. He was appointed to the Senate on January 21, 1901, under the then Liberal government. It was because of his association with Sir William Van Horne that Senator Mackay and his wife came to St. Andrews.

When *Clibrig* was ready for occupancy in the summer of 1906, Senator and Mrs. Mackay moved in. About this time, Sir William Van Horne painted a landscape for his friend, depicting a large birch branch with hills beyond; it is inscribed in the lower right-hand corner to "R.M. from W.C.V.H. 1906." The picture was placed over the fieldstone fireplace in the *Clibrig* dining room. Miss Cairine Wilson, Robert Mackay's granddaughter, later presented it to the Ross Memorial Library.

Opposite: The dining room at the original Clibrig. D. Will McKay

147

The Hon. Senator Cairine Wilson.

Karsh Photo

Jane Baptist Mackay died in 1912, and the senator four years later.

Mr. and Mrs. Robert Loring were the next owners of *Clibrig*. Anna Loring was the daughter of Senator and Mrs. Mackay. She in turn sold the house in 1922 to her sister, Cairine (Mrs. Norman Wilson). Married in 1909, the Wilsons had eight children: Olive, Janet, Cairine, Ralph, Anna, Angus, Robert, and Norma. *Clibrig* was a wonderful place for the children, with its farm, gardens, orchards, the long driveways, and the woods in which to play. The Wilsons were a hospitable family, with many guests, and large Sunday lunches a regular ritual. And of course, the children brought their friends in droves throughout those wonderful summers between the Wars.

Norman Wilson and his wife Cairine were both deeply involved in politics as Liberals. He came from Cumberland, Ontario, and attended the Ontario College of Agriculture in Guelph, maintaining an interest in agriculture and lumbering. Between 1904 and 1908 he sat in the House of Commons as Liberal M.P. for Russell, Ontario. He later became manager of the W.C. Edwards & Company lumber mills. By 1918 the Wilson family had moved from Rockland, Ontario, to Ottawa. In 1925 Norman Wilson again ran as a Liberal candidate in the federal election but was defeated.

Cairine Wilson ventured into politics soon after the move to Ottawa. In 1921, during the federal election campaign, she became joint President of the Eastern Ontario Liberal Association. Later, she became the chief architect of the National Federation of Liberal Women of Canada. In 1930, Mackenzie King appointed her as Canada's first woman senator, and she was the only woman in the Senate for the next five years.

Senator Cairine Wilson's main effort was directed to bringing about a liberalization of Canada's immigration laws. She became the chair of the Central Committee for Interned Refugees in 1941, which had responsibility for enemy aliens from Britain who were brought to Canada in the summer of 1940 and interned in camps. But she also had many interests in organizations outside Parliament.

The Wilsons' house in Ottawa was called the *Manor House*, where Betts, their efficient butler of many years, would welcome their guests in his austere but gracious fashion. He would also accompany the family to St. Andrews and *Clibrig* each summer. Travelling in one of the government private cars, the Wilsons would arrive at the end of June and leave after Labour Day.

Mr. Norman Wilson died in 1956 at the age of eighty, and Senator Cairine Wilson in

1962 at age seventy-seven. St. Andrews remembers them still for the kind things they did for the town. As Presbyterians, they were strong supporters of the Greenock Church. In fact, the Mackays and the Wilsons have been part of St. Andrews life for so long that somehow they are not thought of as being "from away." Olive Wilson, the eldest of their family, who had married Alan Gill of the National Research Council in Ottawa, bought a house and property at Bayside and lived there for several years during the 1950s, until they and their two children moved to Vancouver. Ralph Wilson, who inherited most of the *Clibrig* estate, was the only member of the Wilson family to take up permanent residence in St. Andrews. He and Rowena, his second wife, had their own house at *Clibrig*, originally owned by Charles Burns and his wife, Janet Wilson Burns. Ralph managed the farm until such time as it was considered no longer viable. Like other members of the family, he was a strong supporter of Greenock Church. He died in November 1987.

Norma Wilson Davies was the youngest of the eight Wilson children. She married James I. Davies from Winnipeg. He joined the R.C.A.F. in 1940 and was shot down as a pilot over Germany in 1941, spending the rest of the war in a prison camp. Much later, in 1962, he was appointed Canadian Military Attaché to Israel, where his wife and children accompan-

The original Clibrig, designed by Finley & Spence and built in 1906. D. Will McKay

149

ied him. Retiring from the Service with the rank of Lt.-Gen., he became Vice-President for Governmental Affairs for the De Havilland Division of Boeing Canada. Norma and James Davies had two sons, two daughters, and several grandchildren — the fifth generation of Mackay/Wilson descendants to summer in St. Andrews. They built their own house on the *Clibrig* property in 1973, near the main house, renewing this beautiful estate once again with the sounds of children, dogs, and summer play.

Miss Cairine Wilson was born in 1913, third daughter of Mr. Norman Wilson and Senator Cairine Wilson. After her mother's death in 1962, Miss Cairine Wilson bought the *Clibrig* house in addition to considerable land from the Wilson estate. For ten years she spent her summers in that vast house, usually arriving early in May and staying late in the autumn. *Clibrig* was not winterized and was very cold.

Only Cairine could have done it. With almost no help she entertained family and friends. As you entered *Clibrig*, a large bowl on the long oak table in the main living room was always full of lovely flowers; her flower arrangements were famous, and found not only at *Clibrig* but every Sunday at Greenock Church while she was in residence in St. Andrews. They were also at the Antique Fair held every August and at various House and Garden days.

In 1972, however, it was decided that *Clibrig*, now sixty-seven years old, could no longer be maintained. It was torn down and a new house bearing the same name was built on the same site in 1973, designed by Stanley Emerson of Saint John.

Cairine Wilson never married but she became the central force in the Wilson family, much loved by the younger generation. An excellent golfer and curler, she entered many competitions in both sports. Her generosity was well known. During the Second World War she took three English evacuee children for several years and looked after them wonderfully. For ten years she was president of the Canadian Save the Children Fund and was engaged in countless other good works — being awarded the Order of Canada in 1977 in recognition of what she had accomplished. She was a strong adherent of the Greenock Church in St. Andrews and St. Andrews Presbyterian Church in Ottawa.

But most of all she was great fun. Her friends treasured her friendship. Her life touched many people, and her death in July 1987 brought deep sadness to all who knew her.

Frank MacKenzie Ross

Frank M. Ross bought the stone house and farm in Bayside in 1925. It had been built by John Mowat on original grants of land to two early settlers, Robert Pagan and Dr. Calef, and possessed the most magnificent view of Dochet Island, where Samuel de Champlain wintered in 1604. Frank M. Ross, who was born in 1891, came from the county of Ross and Cromarty in Scotland, and arrived in Canada just before the First World War. He first lived in Saint John and worked as a banker; later he had an interest in the Saint John Dry Docks, being manager at one time. He built *Ashburn Place*, a large house near the city, and married Gertrude Tomalin, from whom he was later divorced. The Crash of 1929 almost ruined Frank M. Ross, but his Scots grit asserted itself and he once again became a rich man.

He bought *Chamcook Farm* four years before the Crash, however, and arranged for his parents, Mr. and Mrs. David Ross, and his two brothers, Alistair and Hugh, to come out from Scotland and live in the modernized house. David Ross — who lost his wife in 1927 — ran the dairy farm until he died in 1934. Hugh had always been delicate, and he died in 1938, at age thirty-four. The graves of Frank M. Ross's parents and his two brothers are in St. Andrews Rural Cemetery.

Frank M. Ross moved to western Canada where he had many business interests; by 1945 he was referred to as a "millionaire industrialist." In that same year he also had the good fortune to marry Phyllis Gregory Turner, the widow of Leonard Turner, who had died in London when Phyllis was only twenty-nine, leaving her with two children: John Napier Turner and Brenda Turner. Phyllis Turner had left London in 1932 and returned with her children to her family in Trail, British Columbia. With her children to support, life was difficult — and there was not much money. But Phyllis Turner was a remarkable woman. Determined and extremely good-looking, she also had a master's degree in Economics. She entered the Civil Service in Ottawa and eventually became chief economist to the Tariff Board, then the highest post held by a woman in the Federal Civil Service. During the Second World War, she

worked for Donald Gordon and the Prices and Trade Board as the Oils and Fats Controller, an important position. She was awarded the C.B.E. for her war service.

In 1955, Frank M. Ross was appointed Lieutenant-Governor of British Columbia, a post he held until 1960, and he and his wife did an exemplary job at Government House in Victoria. Subsequently, Phyllis Ross was elected Chancellor of the University of British Columbia, the first woman university chancellor in the Commonwealth.

After the war, with the children growing up, Frank and Phyllis Ross came to St. Andrews — where they both had many friends — for the summers. For Frank M. Ross, of course, it was a return. By this time the Maxwell house down by the shore had been bought and a cottage built on Chamcook Lake. There was a new tennis court, and the farm had Welsh ponies instead of dairy cows — with beef cattle later on. Mr. and Mrs. Allison Beckerton ran the farm and house for many years, great favourites of the Ross and Turner families and indeed of all their friends.

The Frank M. Ross cottage. Private Collection

It was a wonderful place for young people. Brenda and John had both grown up as attractive and energetic people with lots of friends. Frank and Phyllis Ross were generous and attentive hosts, and there were many dinner parties and guests at *Chamcook Farm*.

John Turner, a Rhodes Scholar, became a lawyer, and married Geills Kilgour of Winnipeg. After extensive political and business experience, he became leader of the Liberal Party, Prime Minister of Canada for a brief period in 1984, and leader of the Parliamentary Opposition through two elections. He and his wife had a daughter Elizabeth and three sons: Michael, David, and Andrew.

Brenda Turner married John Norris, of Montreal, a very well-liked man. They too had three sons and a daughter: Christopher, David, Felicia, and Peter. Brenda Norris served on the board of the Montreal Trust Company, as a governor and also a member of the senate of McGill University, and as a member of the Roosevelt Campobello International Park Commission. She always gave her brother a great deal of support and encouragement in his political career.

Both families have spent many summers in St. Andrews, staying in the *Ross Cottage* down by the shore.

After Frank Ross died on his eightieth birthday in 1971, Phyllis Ross continued to come from Vancouver, where she lived, to St. Andrews. She still enjoyed entertaining and derived the greatest pleasure from her grandchildren. However, her health failed badly during the last six years of her life, and she died on April 19, 1988.

The stone house went to the Norris family, and the white house by the shore to the Turners.

Dr. A.G. Huntsman

Dr. A.G. Huntsman. Private Collection

Dr. and Mrs. Huntsman bought an old hay barn and surrounding land from Robert Bowser in 1948. They converted it into a delightful house two years later. The Huntsmans had been among the early visitors to St. Andrews; they could now spend their summers in their own place.

When marine scientists began to work at St. Andrews in 1899, they had no building to work in, so they lived and worked in a moveable scow with a railway car on top, stationed at Indian Point. This was ingenious, because it could be transported from place to place: to Canso, Nova Scotia (1901-1902); to Malpeque, Prince Edward Island (1903-1904); and to the Gaspé (1905-1907). However, the contraption foundered and was dismantled in 1907.

In 1909 the first building of the St. Andrews Biological Station was constructed at Brandy Cove. It was in use only during the summers. Dr. Archibald Gowanlock Huntsman, already an established scientist, first came to St. Andrews in 1910, returning the next year for a two-year appointment as Curator. Absent during 1916-1919, he became Director in 1919 and held the position until 1934, after which he served as Consulting Director until 1953. During all this period, Dr Huntsman was associated with the Department of Biology at the University of Toronto, where he became Professor of Marine Biology and the best-known Canadian scientist in his field. Miss Madge Rigby of St. Andrews was Dr. Huntsman's secretary and assistant for over thirty years, in Toronto and in the summers in St. Andrews.

In all those years Dr. Huntsman became identified with St. Andrews as few people can be, being instrumental in bringing the Fisheries Research Board to the town, and giving his name to the Huntsman Marine Laboratory — now the Huntsman Marine Science Centre. He thrived on controversy and was a most stimulating leader of research.

But "A.G." was only one of many scientists who visited St. Andrews. In the early years they came for the summer, bringing their wives and children when possible and living at

the Station. However, the scientists and the town community remained to a certain extent separate.

A.G. continued to come to St. Andrews into his old age. In his late eighties he decided to take up bicycling: he was an intimidating sight if he approached you, wobbling down Reed Avenue. Mrs. Huntsman had died some time before, and a grandson, Colin Marchant, often stayed with him during the latter years. Dr. Huntsman died in August 1973, at age ninety.

His daughter, Elinor Mawson, and her husband, Colin, both Ph.Ds themselves, decided to retire to St. Andrews. They lived in A.G.'s house from 1974 to 1982, when it was sold to Mr. and Mrs. Glenwright. The Mawsons then moved to a smaller house on Adolphus Street.

The house of Dr. A.G. Huntsman, Cedar Lane. Private Collection

52

Rossmount, 1889
Destroyed by fire, 1960
Chamcook

Mr. and Mrs. Henry Phipps Ross

In the summer of 1902 a picnic was planned on Chamcook Mountain — and what an important day it proved to be for St. Andrews and Charlotte County! The Rev. and Mrs. Henry Phipps Ross, from the United States, were visiting friends in Robinson, Maine, who suggested a trip to St. Andrews with the picnic to follow. Rev. Ross and his wife readily agreed. Thus it was that two of the greatest benefactors we have ever known in St. Andrews were introduced to the scenic beauty of the area.

The mountain, in addition to eighty-seven acres of land and a house at Chamcook built in 1889, was for sale by James A. Townsend of Brooklyn. The house had been designed by Harry Nelson Black of Saint John and Eastport. It was irresistible and was purchased by the Rosses for $4,500. They renamed the house and estate *Rossmount,* and it became the centre of their lives. Over a number of years, they transformed the interior of the house and laid the extensive flower and vegetable gardens. Frank Adams, a well-known architect from Providence, Rhode Island, was engaged to remodel the house. He built a splendid study for the Rev. Ross at the top of the mansion, and he also laid a new road to Chamcook Mountain. There were huge barns and stables and a carriage house up the hill behind the house.

The Rosses were very welcoming and received many guests and visits from townspeople and summer cottagers. They went on daily trips to scenic places, picnics, clam bakes, lobster boils, and boat outings. Their family and friends were from Boston, New York, and California, and they reached the Chamcook stop by overnight train from Boston, via McAdam.

Rossmount was full of beautiful things — antique furniture, oriental rugs, and a valuable collection of art objects acquired during extensive world travels. The Rev. Ross was an Episcopalian minister, Rector of Taunton, Massachusetts; Providence, Rhode Island; and Palo Alta, California, until his retirement in 1909. Mrs. Ross was the daughter of Charles Finney Clark, President of the Bradstreet Company in New York. In later years the Rosses were active members of the Friends Meeting in Northwest Washington, D.C. When they died within eight days of each other in 1945, they were buried in the St. Andrews Rural Cemetery. Their headstone is a large grey rock, taken from Chamcook Mountain, with a small bronze tablet on which their names and dates are inscribed. It is very simple and somehow very poignant.

In their wills they bequeathed their collection, as well as funding, for the establishment of the Henry Phipps Ross and Sarah Juliet Ross Memorial Museum. They had planned for their museum by buying a large brick house at 188 Montague Street, originally built in 1800 for the Hatch family and called *Chestnut Hall*. In addition, they funded a public library, to be called the Ross Memorial Library. It was built on the lot adjacent to the museum, following the same architectural style.

However, legal complications meant a delay of thirty-two years before these bequests could be implemented. The Ross Library opened in 1977 and the museum in 1980. The Rosses also left a good deal of money to the Charlotte County Hospital in St. Stephen, and the new x-ray unit was named in their memory.

The Rev. and Mrs. Ross had no children but all their lives were particularly kind to young people. In the front hall of the Ross Museum their portraits can be seen, painted by Mary Curtis Richardson. They were both small and not distinctive-looking people, yet great kindness shines from their faces. At Christmas, each room at the museum is decorated around a special theme, and the building is full of children. The library, too, has a fine children's program, and both museum and library have thousands of visitors each year. Rev. and Mrs. Ross used their wealth with care to enrich the lives of many in St. Andrews and beyond.

After the death of the Rosses, *Rossmount* was bought by Mr. John Syme of Saint John, who ran it as a hotel called *Rossmount Inn*. Sadly, it burned down in 1960. Because of the terms of the insurance, the owners had to rebuild to the same size, but it was not, alas, a graceful replica. After that the house had several owners, all of whom have made improvements and developed the *Rossmount* as a fine inn and restaurant.

Sarah Juliet Ross and Rev. Henry Phipps Ross. Ross Memorial Museum

53

Delmar Leighton

Mr. and Mrs. Delmar Leighton, of Cambridge, Massachusetts, built their summer house in 1934 next to the old Mowat farm house, called *Beech Hill,* and the home of Miss Grace Helen Mowat. Born in 1897, Del Leighton originally came from Pennsylvania. After serving in the First World War as a pilot in the Marine Flying Corps, he returned to Harvard, where he went on to study economics. He married Isabella Carr (Dolly) Thompson in 1925 and they had three children: Isabella Carr (Polly), Andrew, and Delmar Jr. (Tim).

Harvard President A.L. Lowell recognized Delmar Leighton's special abilities and appointed him the first Dean of Freshmen at the university, a position he held for thirty-six years. So successful was he that he became known as the "Dean of Deans." After taking several other positions, he retired in 1963. Only three years later, on May 13, 1966, he died while working in his St. Andrews garden.

Dolly Leighton and her brother Lovell Thompson first came to St. Andrews with their grandparents, Mr. and Mrs. Lucien Carr, from St. Louis, Missouri, and their parents, Mr. and Mrs. Charles Miner Thompson, in 1908. In 1989, Dolly Leighton held the record for all summer visitors to St. Andrews, coming for eighty years.

The Carrs and Thompsons were interesting families. Mr. Lucien Carr was born in Troy, Missouri, in 1829. He studied at a Jesuit college and then graduated with a B.A. from St. Louis University. Showing marked literary abilities, he first turned to journalism and worked for the *Missouri Republican.* In 1854 he married Miss Cornelia Louisa Crow, later abandoning journalism for health reasons and moving east with his wife in 1867 to live in Cambridge, Massachusetts, which was to remain their home for the rest of their lives. He had developed a great interest in the study of North American Indians and in American archeology, and became recognized as an authority in these fields. Between 1877 and 1894 he acted as assistant curator of the Peabody Museum of Archeology and Ethnology at Harvard, publishing extensively on his chosen subjects.

Dolly Leighton's father, Charles Miner Thompson, was born in Montpelier, Vermont, in 1864, and married Isabella Wayman Carr in 1898. A graduate of Harvard (class of 1886), he worked for a few years as a reporter on the *Boston Daily Advertiser* and later as literary editor. During the 1930s he was an editor for the Harvard University Press, the author of several books, and the translator of books by Georges Clemenceau and Georges Duhamel.

When Mrs. Lucien Carr first came to St. Andrews in 1908, she and the Thompson family all stayed at the Grimmer house, later the Anglican rectory, which they rented each summer until 1911. But Mrs. Carr also took a great liking to the Mowat farm and bought it in 1908 with the provision that George Mowat and his daughter, Grace Helen Mowat, could live there for their lifetimes. George Mowat died in 1917 at the age of ninety-one, and his daughter lived to be eighty-nine and died in 1964. Mrs. Carr had planned to build a large house, similar to Senator Mackay's *Clibrig* (1906), on this beautiful piece of land. But of course it never happened. Dolly Leighton said that they never regretted the arrangement they had made with the Mowats. Grace Helen Mowat was a remarkable woman and the three Leighton children took part in everything going on at her house. There was great activity, especially during the thirties and forties — weaving, watching the wool being dyed, country fairs, fiddlers, and square dancing. As Dolly Leighton remarked: "A whole education in itself!" In all this, the most important element was Miss Mowat herself — and no one could ever forget her.

So the Thompson family just went on renting different houses each summer; in 1912 it was Prof. Emery Hoar's house, later *Tara Manor*; between 1913 and 1916, *Chestnut Hall* (now the Ross Memorial Museum); 1917, the Wheelock (later the Oppe) house; in 1918, Miss Morris' (later the Jacqueline Davis) house. Then there were a number of interrupted years. Later, until they built their own house, Dolly and Del Leighton often stayed with Miss Elizabeth (Beth) Smith.

Lovell Thompson, Dolly Leighton's brother, graduated from Harvard in 1925 and later joined the publishing firm of Houghton Mifflin, rising from editorial work to become president of the Houghton Mifflin trade department. In his latter years, at an age when most men would rest on their laurels, he started his own small but successful publishing house, Gambit Press. Like his sister, Lovell Thompson spent many childhood summers in St. Andrews, and after Miss Grace Mowat died in 1964, he came with his own family to stay at the Mowat farmhouse.

At our local post office, the postmaster sometimes referred to the arrival of our summer visitors as the "Robins Returning." After eighty years, Mrs. Delmar Leighton was certainly one of the most familiar ones! But like a true New Englander she would never sentimentalize about St. Andrews in the ways that make local people squirm. She knew that the beauty of the town conceals a real working life. As a child her hero was Mr. John Andrew Doon (Eldon Doon's father), and her ambition was to work on his fish pier, wearing his rubber boots and slicker. She recalled how kind he was to her, letting her turn the drying fish on the flats and investigate the daily catch. That simple magic remained in later years, perhaps heightened when her daughter Polly, who married Dr. Cheves Smythe, came in the summers, drawing her five grown sons from various parts of the United States with their wives and children. In addition, Andrew Leighton came from Cambridge, Massachusetts, with his wife, Phebe, a landscape architect, and their children and grandchildren. Sadly, Delmar Leighton Jr. (Tim), who loved sailing on the bay and spent so much time at their camp in Bocabec, was missing; he died of leukemia on January 13, 1975, at age forty-four.

The Leightons are now into their sixth generation as St. Andrews summer visitors. The exterior of the old dark red Mowat farm house, next door to the house that Delmar and Dolly Leighton built in 1934 (now called *Beech Hill*), has changed very little, although the tall elms that surrounded it had to be felled because of Dutch elm disease. There is, however, one great change. Now twelve or more people live in the house each summer; it rings with the cries of children and with the sounds of young men and women enjoying themselves in a place they have known since childhood.

C.S. Everett and E.W.T. Gill

This house on Edward Street, which Mr. and Mrs. C.S. Everett bought in 1891, had originally been built about 1825. It was a small brick building in those days; several years later, two brothers, John and Edward Wilson, bought and enlarged it. In 1865 Edward Wilson then left this charming house in his will to his housekeeper, Miss Lucy Sprague. She kept a genteel boarding house for gentlemen for many years and lived to a great age.

When C.S. Everett purchased the house, he was living in Saint John. He made considerable alterations to the brick house, with further enlargements, and also finished the top storey. The new and extremely graceful half-circular porch over the front door, with pillars and balustrade above, was designed by a gifted local contractor called Mr. Stoddard. These changes took time and the Everett family did not move from Saint John until 1902.

Dr Herbert Everett and Douglas Everett were the sons of C.S. Everett and his wife. After their parents died, they sold *Maplehurst* to Mrs. Jura Hall, of Berkeley, California (originally of St. Louis, Missouri) in 1936. Mrs. Hall had been a friend of the McKittrick Jones family in St. Louis and had visited them in St. Andrews at their house on De Monts Road. During the twenty-five years that Mrs. Hall owned *Maplehurst*, it was rented several times. In 1934, their Excellencies the Earl and Countess of Bessborough rented it for their children for the summer. Mrs. Jura Hall's daughter-in-law, Ann Walsh Hall, became a permanent resident of St. Andrews, where before her marriage she spent all her summers with her father, L.O.P. Walsh, in the former Macklem house on Reed Avenue.

Mrs. Jura Hall sold *Maplehurst* in 1961 to Evan and Dorothy Gill. Evan Gill was with the Department of External Affairs, serving in London, South Africa, Ghana, Australia, and Ireland. As he was Canadian High Commissioner in Australia, and Canadian ambassador to Ireland from 1965 to his retirement in 1968, he and his wife were not able to take up residence in St. Andrews until then. However, the Gill family members were no strangers to the town. Born in 1902, Evan Gill first came to St. Andrews as a summer visitor with his parents, Mr. and Mrs. Robert Gill of Ottawa, about 1908.

Members of the Gill family, c. 1928.
Left to right (back row): Henry Gill;
his wife Vera; Evan; (seated) Mr. and Mrs.
Robert Gill; (front) Francis. Private Collection.

Opposite: Maplehurst; original house
built in 1825. Chris Fleming

Evan Gill's mother had been Ann Louisa Thistle, one of three attractive Thistle sisters from Aylmer, Quebec. Her uncle, Sir Henry Egan, had big lumber interests. Louisa Thistle had visited St. Andrews with Sir Henry and Lady Egan soon after the *Algonquin Hotel* opened in 1889 and stayed there with them in 1902.

Her husband, Robert Gill, was a banker in Ottawa with the Canadian Imperial Bank of Commerce. Mr. and Mrs. Gill had three sons: Henry, Evan, and Francis. When they first brought their children to St. Andrews, they rented the *Anchorage* on Parr Street, then owned by Capt. and Mrs. Frederick G. Andrews. When Robert Gill retired from the bank in 1911, the Gills bought *Hillside*, the first summer cottage built in St. Andrews (by Robert S. Gardiner), from Mr. Gardiner's daughter, Mrs. Alice Payne. *Hillside* was renamed *Gillcairn*, and plans for an addition and other alterations were made by Edward Maxwell.

Robert Gill loved to play golf, and one of his good golfing friends was David R. Forgan. Not only did they derive pleasure from the game itself but they also wrote poetical epitaphs about their failures. Towards the end of his life Robert Gill unfortunately lost his sight. He died in 1929.

The three sons were all married: Henry to Vera Birkett, Evan to Dorothy (Do) Laurie, and Francis to Betty Fauquier. The Gills were a delightful and united family, with their widowed mother very much at the head of it, and since the wives enjoyed St. Andrews as much as their husbands did, *Gillcairn* soon became a haven for grandchildren too. After Mrs. Gill's death the house was owned jointly by her sons. It was often rented, but usually one of the three Gill families occupied it for the summer. It was sold in 1956, after the Gills had owned it for forty-five years, to Gen. and Mrs. James A. Van Fleet, of Florida.

But St. Andrews must have made its special mark on Evan and Do Gill with their acquisition of *Maplehurst*. They were much loved and admired in the town, and their daughter, Louisa O'Reilly, and their sons, Evan and Christopher, spent their childhoods in St. Andrews. Eleven grandchildren have either visited or worked at summer jobs in the town — and great-grandchildren now make the Gills one of our five-generation families.

Sir William Van Horne

Sir William Cornelius Van Horne was one of the most industrious and dynamic men in Canada, and famous as the builder of the Canadian Pacific Railway. Sir William bought six hundred acres of land on the western end of Minister's Island as early as 1891, eight years before he retired as President of the C.P.R. His plans for the house were grandiose, with extensive landscaping, large barns, and a tower bathhouse with a saltwater swimming pool among the red rocks below. By 1893 an army of men were at work making roads and building the foundation of the house and a special windmill to pump water. Although Sir William began as his own architect, there were many complications, and in 1898-1899 the young Montreal architect Edward Maxwell was asked to come to St. Andrews to redraft some of the plans. This Maxwell did, and the work then went ahead smoothly to its completion in 1901.

By land, *Covenhoven* could be reached only by a sandbar exposed at low tide — meaning that the island was cut off twice daily — and Sir William and Lady Van Horne enjoyed its seclusion. They came for many summers, travelling in their C.P.R. railcar, the *Saskatchewan*, and leaving the St. Andrews train at the little Bar Road station, where carriages from *Covenhoven* would meet them. (There were no automobiles on the island in Sir William's day.)

The *Saskatchewan* was no ordinary railcar. Built specially for Sir William in 1883, it was used for all his railway travelling. The interior was mahogany and lit by brass lamps. The master bedroom had a brass bedstead fastened to the floor. It was in this elegant vehicle that Sir William, Donald Smith, and Sanford Fleming journeyed on a rainy, misty day to Craigellachie, between Sicamous and Revelstoke, British Columbia. On the following day, November 7, 1885, the last spike of the C.P.R. was driven in by Donald Smith in a simple ceremony attended only by Van Horne, Fleming, and a small crowd of railway workers. Sir William's speech on that occasion was brief and to the point: "All I can say is that the work has been well done in every way." But it was a C.P.R. conductor who summed up this historic occasion best by crying out, "All aboard for the Pacific!"

Opposite: The barn at Covenhoven. C.P.R.

Sir William Van Horne. C.P.R.

Much later, the *Saskatchewan* was renamed the *Quebec*, and later just plain Number 38. When it was withdrawn from service, it was donated by the company to the Canadian Railroad Historical Association as a personal monument to Sir William Van Horne.

On Minister's Island, Sir William became a gentleman farmer. He imported a herd of Dutch Belted black and white cattle. His barns and stables were huge; everything was spotless; the men who worked in the barns wore long white lab coats, and each day, at the end of work, they had to spread fresh sawdust on the floors. There were also large greenhouses where grapes and peaches were grown, while beautiful flowers filled the large stone urns placed along the driveway to the house, which was itself surrounded by flower beds. Harry Clarke was the expert gardener. With the bar covered at high tide it was, of course, necessary to have a boat. Capt. John O'Halloran was master of the *Covenhoven*, Sir William's twenty-horsepower motor-launch, and he also skippered the sailing yacht *Uvira*. Among those who worked at *Covenhoven,* a number remarked on the kindliness and friendliness of Sir William and Lady Van Horne.

The Van Hornes were always accompanied by their daughter, Miss Adeline, affectionately known as Miss Addie. She was over six feet tall and very large, like her father — whom she was like in other ways too. She had an excellent brain for business and Sir William often relied upon her good judgement. Educated at a boarding school in Berlin for several years, she became a student of geology — again following her father, as she did in her skill at the identification of mushrooms.

Later on, the Van Hornes' son, Richard Benedict (Bennie) Van Horne, his wife (the former Edith Molson), and their son William Cornelius Covenhoven Van Horne, also came for summer visits. But while Sir William had a great love for all his family, he was especially fond of Billy, his only grandchild. He spoiled him unashamedly, and when travelling he sent the boy a postcard every day, some of which he sketched, depicting himself frequently as an elephant.

Apart from his feats as a builder of railways, Sir William was a knowledgeable and experienced collector of art, possessing one of the finest collections in North America. In addition to paintings, he also collected Chinese and Japanese porcelain, while many of the great artists of the world — such as Rembrandt, Frans Hals, Goya, and Renoir, to name but a few — were hung on the walls of his house on Sherbrooke Street, Montreal, and at *Covenhoven*. Sir William only bought paintings he genuinely liked. He said "the purchase of a painting is like the selection of a wife — never have one that you're not in love with."

A gifted amateur painter himself, he found painting a great relaxation, being known to paint late at night and into the early hours of the morning. He sometimes painted in St. Andrews with George Inness, the American artist, and William Hope, whose house, *Dalmeny*, was on the Bar Road.

The Van Hornes were very generous about allowing visitors to drive around their house and gardens. Children of the 1920s recalled with nostalgia Mr. William McQuoid's surrey with the fringe on top and Doctor, his black horse. A rare treat was to visit the Van Horne island, riding in this hired carriage for the afternoon. Mr. McQuoid could always judge the tide correctly, but it was a bit frightening to be driven across the bar when the water was not really off — it came up to the hubs of the narrow wheels and the gravel was so slippery.

Sir William and Lady Van Horne enjoyed entertaining and gave several large parties each summer. One guest recalled being asked by Sir William if he wanted milk or champagne to drink as "they both cost the same on this island" — referring, of course, to his herd of expensive Dutch Belted cattle. When the Van Hornes were not on the island, a large staff remained there to maintain *Covenhoven*, the gardens, and the farm. Bill Clarke, son of Harry Clarke, the head gardener, also lived and worked on the island and loved to talk about those great days. Peaches and grapes from the greenhouses, vegetables, butter and cream from the dairy, all would be boxed and taken to the Bar Road station, there to be loaded on the train for delivery to the Sherbrooke Street house in Montreal early next morning.

Sir William Van Horne resigned as President of the C.P.R. on June 12, 1899, although he remained a Director and Chairman of the Board and only retired from the company in May 1910. He had been knighted in 1894, receiving the K.C.M.G.

There was really no retirement for Sir William, such was his zest for life. Besides *Covenhoven*, he owned four thousand acres in Selkirk, Manitoba, which he had purchased in 1898, and where he grew wheat, bred cattle, and farmed on the grand scale. In 1900, he became President of the Cuba Company Railroad, with headquarters in New York. This required frequent visits to Cuba. There were also many other business interests in addition to the trips abroad to add to his art collections. He also loved good food. In Europe he patronized only the best restaurants, and it gave him great amusement when sometimes, travelling in France, he was mistaken for King Edward VII. The likeness can plainly be seen in photographs.

There are many photographs of Sir William. He was very photogenic. One of the best

Miss Adeline Van Horne. Photo found in the Boy Scout Hall, St. Andrews.

Notman Photo, McCord Museum

Covenhoven, residence of Sir William Van Horne on Minister's Island. Designed by Sir William Van Horne. C.P.R.

shows him sitting in his favourite office chair; it had no arms and he liked to sit on it backwards, as if on a saddle. He placed his comfortable stomach against its back, rested his elbows on it, smoked a cigar, and talked. The chair had hard usage — not only was Sir William a massive man but when he got up to show something to a visitor, he would often kick the chair aside.

Many people have said that Canadians today have little knowledge of what Sir William Van Horne achieved for the country. This President and General Manager of the C.P.R. was no ordinary chief executive sitting in a plush office suite far from the scene of operations. For example, in 1884 Van Horne and his party had just arrived at the Mountain Creek Trestle of the still incomplete C.P.R. line. He was told that just a few days before, several men had crashed to their deaths in the ravine below. The floor of the trestle, suspended 160 feet above the torrent, consisted at that time of two loose planks and nothing more. One companion accompanying Van Horne was barely able to cross the bridge by crawling, inch by inch, on his hands and knees. But the General Manager stepped out onto the shaky planks full of confidence. He strode across the trestle and returned the same way. No one could say that he lacked the courage of his great engineering vision.

Sir William Van Horne died on September 11, 1915, three weeks after a stomach operation. He was seventy-two. His last wish, it is said, expressed the same energy with which he had lived all his life: "When I think of all I could do, I should like to live five hundred years." He was buried in Joliet, Illinois, where he had spent his youth, and his body was taken there by the railcar *Saskatchewan*.

Minister's Island and *Covenhoven* were purchased eventually by the Province of New Brunswick. The house which Sir William and Lady Van Horne loved so much is lonely and in need of repairs. Their Montreal house was bulldozed to the ground in 1973.

Sir William Van Horne was a great and remarkable man; and in St. Andrews we think of him as one of us. We are proud of this and boast of it.

After Sir William's death, Miss Adeline continued to come to *Covenhoven* with her mother. "Miss Addie" ran everything — the house, the farm, the large staff. Both she and her mother were dressed in mourning black for many years. Miss Adeline's long, full dresses made her look even larger than she was, but her size was truly formidable. The first Model T Ford she bought — a grand affair with lamps on both sides — had to have a special very large door made to enable her to climb in and out. Dreyer, the coachman, had to learn to drive, much against his will, and become the chauffeur.

In earlier years, Dreyer had driven his mistress to St. Andrews by buckboard, when the tide was off the bar. The seats went across the carriage and Miss Adeline would sit at the back while her guests took the front seats. The first stop would be at the post office, and then down the street to O'Neill's grocery store, where Mr. Henry O'Neill would come out to meet such a distinguished customer and receive from her the grocery list prepared by her housekeeper or cook. Several Model Ts followed the buckboard until Miss Adeline finally bought a Cadillac — custom-made, with a specially reinforced body. At this point it was decided that Dreyer really was not up to driving such an expensive car, and Mr. Lefèvre of Montreal became the new chauffeur. Later Miss Adeline bought a Rolls Royce for use in Montreal — buying it mainly to surprise her brother, Richard Benedict (Bennie).

Miss Adeline enjoyed entertaining the townspeople and gave a picnic for them on the island every summer. On August 7, 1930, the Ayrshire Breeders Annual Field Day was held there, with three hundred people in attendance, and the town's Boy Scout troop camped on Minister's Island. Miss Adeline's interest in the Boy Scout Association began when her nephew, Billy Van Horne, became a Scout at the age of eleven, later becoming a King's Scout. In 1930 she donated a small hall and gymnasium to the local Scouts. It was built on Prince of Wales Street near the Loyalist Burial Ground and opened that year by Lady Willingdon.

Memories of Miss Adeline have been overshadowed by those of her famous father, of the eccentric behaviour and life of her brother, and of the wildness and irresponsibility of her nephew. But she was an outstanding lady. Intelligent and well educated, she could have been a fine botanist or geologist. Perhaps because of her size, she is remembered as being rather shy; nevertheless, she could be very much at ease with people, especially the young.

Carmelita O'Neill O'Hagan, of Vancouver, British Columbia, and Mary O'Neill Thompson, of Woodstock, New Brunswick, daughters of Mr. and Mrs. Alphonsus (Phonsie) O'Neill, remembered Miss Adeline well. When they were girls they were often invited to tea at *Covenhoven*. In 1933, Carmelita O'Neill started her training as a nurse at the Royal Victoria Hospital in Montreal, and Miss Van Horne invited her to Christmas dinner at the house on Sherbrooke Street. One did not feel shy with Miss Adeline: she did most of the talking and loved to describe and show off all the beautiful paintings her father had collected; she knew everything about them. Mary O'Neill also remembered going to lunch with Miss Adeline in Montreal a few years later. Since Miss Adeline's eyesight was fading fast by this time, she told Mary O'Neill how she insisted, after the paintings were cleaned, that they be put back precisely where they had been. Though she found it difficult to see them now, she knew their positions and could describe them in detail.

The King and Queen visited Montreal at the end of May 1939. Knowing that Carmelita O'Neill and Harry O'Hagan were to be married in August that year, Miss Adeline invited them to come to the balcony of the Sherbrooke Street house to watch the royal entourage drive past. She had many other guests that day, but she included the young couple because she knew and liked them — and because they represented the well-known O'Neill family of St. Andrews that had close ties with the Van Hornes.

Miss Van Horne was a Unitarian. (It is not known with what other denominations the Van Horne family had connections, as very little mention is made of their church affiliation.) She died in 1941 at the age of seventy-three and was buried, like both her parents, at Joliet, Illinois. St. Andrews still remembers Miss Addie, but perhaps it was never fully realized what a capable and worthy successor she had been to her illustrious father.

Miss Adeline's brother, known as Bennie, was born on May 21, 1877, and was thus nine years younger than his sister. He married Edith Molson of Montreal. Sir William Van Horne was pleased with this marriage, as the Molsons were a distinguished Montreal family, and his joy was great when his only grandchild was born in 1907 and named William Cornelius Covenhoven Van Horne.

Bennie Van Horne and his wife Edith, with their son Billy, were frequent visitors to *Covenhoven*. Bennie loved to party and also loved to drink. A story is told that Capt. O'Halloran had to wait many a night at the end of Market wharf with the *Covenhoven*, the Van Horne motor-launch, while Bennie enjoyed a party on shore at the hotel or casino. One night Bennie arrived very late and rather the worse for wear. Capt. O'Halloran was very tired and fed up. He let his master take one step on board then quickly accelerated so that Richard Benedict Van Horne fell to the deck.

William (Billy) Cornelius Covenhoven Van Horne, grandson of Sir William Van Horne, aged three years.

Notman Photo, McCord Museum

Bennie inherited some of his father's artistic talent but unfortunately never did anything about it. He was a very good cartoonist and had an amazing ability to catch a likeness; sometimes the name of someone he had met travelling or at dinner would escape him, yet he could draw a perfect sketch from memory — occasionally on a napkin or tablecloth.

Sir William made him Vice-President, then President, of the Cuba Company Railroad, which necessitated his living in New York for sixteen years. During that time his chauffeur, Sammy Taylor, became his friend and companion. In the late 1920s, Bennie bought a huge yacht called the *Intrepid*, which had a crew of twenty-seven and cost $1,500,000. It was brought to St. Andrews for one summer.

Bennie Van Horne died in 1931 at the age of fifty-four. He was staying at *Covenhoven* at the time and was buried in the St. Andrews Rural Cemetery. His wife was remarried the following year to Robert Randolph Bruce, former Lieutenant-Governor of British Columbia. They

Ownership of *Covenhoven* since 1961

1961 Bought by an Ohio syndicate, which built an airstrip.

1971 Charlie Van Horne, the first Minister of Tourism in New Brunswick and no relation to Sir William, obtained an option on the property. However, he failed to persuade Premier Hatfield and the then Conservative government to purchase the property for $400,000. A few months later, Norman Langdon, a New England developer, bought the island, reputedly for $325,000. He spent approximately $300,000 repairing the barn, roads, house, etc., and renamed the property *Harbour Farm*.

1977 Norman Langdon offered the property to the New Brunswick government, which was again uninterested. He announced his intention of holding an auction. An auction of the house and what remained of the contents was held on March 12-13, 1977. Alexander George and Michael McPherson purchased the island. Three days after

(continued opposite)

were married at *Covenhoven* by the Rev. Dr. Wardlow Taylor, minister of Greenock Church. Mr. Bruce later became Canadian Minister to Japan from 1936 to 1938.

Richard Benedict Van Horne's only son, William Cornelius Covenhoven Van Horne, was born in 1907, and as Sir William Van Horne's only grandchild became the recipient of an intense and perhaps finally destructive love. Sir William was a very loving family man who had taken care of his mother all her life and then his sister. In turn, he spoiled his grandson Billy beyond reason, giving him every kind of toy imaginable. Old men who had gone to school with Billy at Selwyn House School, Montreal, remembered being invited to the Van Horne house to play. Sir William had set up an entire model railway in one of the large rooms — a boy's idea of heaven in those days. However, Billy was bored with it, threw things around, and took his pals elsewhere.

Capt. Maloney of St. Andrews was an expert craftsman and maker of model ships. Sir William would order six or more at a time for his grandson, who would float them on the *Covenhoven* lily pond and use them as targets for his toy guns. When they had been all sunk or sufficiently battered, more would be ordered. Someone asked Capt. Maloney if he felt bad about this. He replied, "No, I don't. I have to make a living and this is one way I do it."

Billy married, and he and his wife had one child, a daughter named Beverley Ann. She was only a baby when her mother was killed in a tragic car accident in St. Andrews on August 16, 1934. The family had come to stay at *Covenhoven* three weeks earlier. Billy Van Horne married again, this time Margaret Hannon — who was also nicknamed Billy — from Montreal. She was a very good wife to her difficult husband and a kind stepmother to Ann.

Around 1936, they built a large log cabin at the eastern end of Minister's Island, called *Moose Manor*. It started with just one room and was later extended. They liked to live there during the summers and to go there with their friends during the hunting season.

Fairly rapidly, however, alcohol dragged down William Cornelius Covenhoven Van Horne. He and his wife bought the Thomas O'Dell house at 88 Augusta Street in St. Andrews and spent most of the Second World War there. For a time Billy tried to work for the Navy at Cornwallis, Nova Scotia, but that ended in failure. He was often seen at the end of the St. Andrews wharf, wearing some sort of naval cap and equipped with both telescope and binoculars. He spent most of his days looking for German submarines.

Some time before this, Sydney Ivor (Pat) Pethick became Billy's chauffeur — you could almost say bodyguard, since he certainly kept him out of a lot of trouble. But Billy needed more than this kind of protection and died in 1946 in Montreal at the age of thirty-nine. He was buried beside his father, Richard Benedict, under a huge tombstone in the St. Andrews Rural Cemetery. For some sad reason, however, neither his wife nor his daughter ever arranged for his name to be engraved on the stone.

So Billy Van Horne rests without memorial. But his friends in St. Andrews and those who worked for him remembered his kindness and generosity. He was a true Van Horne in that respect.

After Billy's death, Pat Pethick lived in the Rev. Andrews's original stone house on Minister's Island, where the Royal Trust had appointed him to run the farm, the house, and the property. Beverley Ann inherited the estate and visited a few times when her children were small. But *Covenhoven* was too large and she made the decision to sell the island and everything else. It has been bought and sold several times since that sale in 1961 and was purchased in 1982 by the Province of New Brunswick.

(continued)

the auction, the New Brunswick government belatedly placed the house and its contents under the Historic Sites Protection Act. Most of the Van Horne furnishings had been sold, however.

1982 The Province of New Brunswick purchased the property from Alexander George and Michael McPherson.

Finale

And now my story ends! But I would like to pay a special tribute that doesn't end – to the real people of St. Andrews, the ones who live here all year round and have seen so many summer visitors, so many old friends, come and go. The town has been greatly blessed with gifts and fine buildings. But its people have retained their own character and independence, living in a place where men and women are judged on their merits and not by their worldly goods.

Many people gave generously to the preparation of this book, and I would like to express my particular gratitude to: Elinor Mawson, archivist of the Charlotte County Archives, who suggested that I write this book; E.H. Snell and Irene Scarratt, Curators of Photographs at the archives; William McMullon and Frank Cunningham, St. Andrews Biological Station, Graphics Division; Rose Haughn, for the use of many photographs by her father, D. Will McKay; the C.P.R. Corporate Archives; the Notman Photographic Archives, McCord Museum, McGill University; Margot Mais and Lord Shaughnessy (family albums); the Murray Vaughan family (photographs); David Freeman (D.R. Forgan albums); Janet Davies (Norman Wilson photographs); Elaine Ross and Margaret MacNichol, research with early St. Andrews newspapers and key materials; Harry Mallory, vital as chief historical advisor; Janet Stewart, typist and valued critic; J.W. Frise, Manager of the *Algonquin*, who gave help and encouragement from the beginning; the St. Andrews Civic Trust, for granting $1,000 toward project costs; and the owners, and families of former owners, of the houses described in these pages, for their great help, cooperation, and patience in answering my many questions.

My husband, David Walker, has given me great support and invaluable criticism.

Willa Walker

St. Andrews Summer Houses, 1870-1950

Wherever known, this list includes map index number, name of owner, domicile, date of building or of its purchase as a summer cottage, architect, name and location of cottage, and some details of later ownership.

1. Thompson, F.W.; Montreal (1909). Architect: Edward Maxwell. *Meadow Lodge*. At the top of Harriet Street off Prince of Wales Street. Later owned by Mr. Maxwell Pascal, Montreal; Lady Beaverbrook. Purchased in 1977 by Mr. and Mrs. John Findlay, Fredericton.

2. Inness, George Jr.; New York (1893). *Lazy Croft*. At Acadia and Prince of Wales streets. Later owned by Mr. George Hopkins, New York; his daughter, Mrs. Hobart Johnson, Wisconsin; Mr. and Mrs. Thomas Shaughnessy, Montreal. Destroyed by fire in 1972.

3. Shaughnessy, Sir Thomas; Montreal (1902). *The Fort*. On Prince of Wales Street. Later owned by the Hon. Marguerite Shaughnessy; the Hon. Mrs. Redmond; Mr. and Mrs. Norman Mais. Purchased in 1985 by the Province of New Brunswick.

4. Hosmer, Charles R.; Montreal (1905). Architect: Edward Maxwell. *Hillcrest*. On Prince of Wales Street. Later owners: Miss Olive Hosmer, Montreal: Mrs.

Donald Oland, Halifax; Mr. and Mrs. Carol Dooley, St. Stephen and Bermuda; Mr. and Mrs. Donald Lamarre, Quebec; Mr. and Mrs. Charles Khoury, Fredericton.

5. Smith, Charles F.; Montreal (1907). Architect: Edward Maxwell. *Rosemount*. On Prince of Wales Street. Later owned by Mr. Edward MacKay, Montreal; Mrs. Anna Reay Cundill; the Hosmer Estate.

6. Markey, Mr. F.H.; Montreal (1910). Architect: Edward Maxwell. *Cliffside*. At the top of King Street. Remodelled in 1951 by Mr. A. Murray Vaughan and Mrs. Marguerite Vaughan Eller and renamed *Les Goélands*.

7. McMaster, Donald; Montreal (1898). *Kingsbrae*. At the top of King Street. Later owned by Percy Cowans, Montreal; Mr. and Mrs. Howard Pillow, Montreal. Torn down in 1971.

8. Wheelock, Mr. T.R.; Shanghai (1897). At the top of King Street. Later owned by their daughter, Mrs. F. Ayscough MacNair; Mr. and Mrs. Robert

Struthers, Norton, Connecticut; Mrs. James Oppe.

9. Heney, Theodore; Montreal (c. 1860). *Pippincott*. At King and Prince of Wales streets. Original house owned by the Lamb family. Later owned by Dr. and Mrs. Bryan Spires; Mr. Robert Parke.

10. Cowan, Charles; Ottawa (c. 1908). Architect: F. Neill Brodie. 88 Augusta Street. Built by Thomas O'Dell. Later owned by William (Billy) Van Horne, grandson of Sir William; Hugh A. Plumstead; Mrs. Edna Price; Dr. R.H. Cook.

11. Smith, Jeremiah; Cambridge, Massachusetts (1915). Architect: John W. Ames, Cambridge, Massachusetts. On Acadia Road. Later owned by Prof. Smith's sister, Miss Elizabeth H. Smith, Cambridge, Massachusetts; Mr. and Mrs. Louis Kronenberger and family, Brookline, Massachusetts.

12. Smoot, Lewis Egerton; Washington, D.C. (1929). *Dayspring*. On De Monts Road. Later owned by Sir James

Dunn and Lady Dunn (later Lady Beaverbrook).

13. Dodd, Robert; Montreal (1930). Architect: W. S. Maxwell & Pitts. On De Monts Road. Later owned by Lady Davis, Montreal. Redesigned by Maxwell & Pitts in 1943. Later owned by Lady Beaverbrook.

14. Seely, Douglas B.; Montreal (1912). On De Monts Road. Later owned by L.M.C. Sams, Toronto; Lady Beaverbrook. Torn down in 1976.

15. Southam, Mr. H.S.; Ottawa (1913). On De Monts Road. Later owned by Mr. and Mrs. McKittrick Jones, St. Louis, Missouri; Mr. and Mrs. Norman Mais, who called it *Malahide*; Mrs. E.M. O'Donnell.

16. Gardiner, Robert S.; Boston (1893). On De Monts Road (upper side). First summer cottage to be built specifically in St. Andrews. Plans for alterations completed by Edward Maxwell in 1915. Later owned by Mr. and Mrs. Robert Gill, Ottawa, and called *Gillcairn*; Gen. and Mrs. James Van Fleet, Florida; Dempsie Van Fleet McChristian (Gen. Van Fleet's daughter) and her husband, Maj.-Gen. McChristian, Hobe Sound, Florida.

17. Forgan, David R.; Chicago (1888-1889). *Berwick Brae*. At the corner of Elizabeth and Carleton streets. Bought by Mr. and Mrs. David R. Forgan in 1900, it had been moved from the St. Andrews Land Company Eastern Commons. Extensive alterations and additions were then made. Later owned by James MacFarlane, St. Andrews; Mr. and Mrs. George Durgan, St. Andrews. Purchased in 1971 and extensively renovated by Mr. and Mrs. John Cowans, formerly of Montreal.

18. Cobb, Edward H.; Cambridge, Massachusetts (1900). At Elizabeth and Carleton streets. Later owned by the Ganong family, Toronto; Hebert M. Stuart; Mrs. Laura Markey; Mrs. Catherine Walsh; Mr. and Mrs. Feeney; Mrs. Barbara Rea; Dr. and Mrs. John Carrothers.

19. Reed, Hayter (1912). Architect: Charles Sax. *Pansy Patch*. On Carleton Street. Later owned by Mr. S.F. Houston, Philadelphia; Mr. and Mrs. H.D. Burns, Toronto; Mr. and Mrs. John Gale, Montreal; Mr. Allen M. Balliet and Mrs. Helen L. Balliet, Shippensburg, Pennsylvania, and Machias, Maine; Mr. and Mrs. Michael Lazare, New Milford, Connecticut.

20. Reed, Gordon; Montreal (c. 1830; rebuilt c. 1915). *Cory Cottage*. On Carleton Street next door to *Pansy Patch*. Purchased in 1960 by Judge John F. Kelly, Cohoes, New York.

21. Tilley, Sir Leonard (1871). *Linden Grange*. On Carleton Street between Edward and William streets. Alterations and additions made in 1921, when purchased for Miss Olive Hosmer by C.R. Hosmer. Later owned by Miss May Spurge; Mrs. Margaret Heenan; the Heenan family, Montreal.

22. Everett, C.S. (1891; original house built in 1825). *Maplehurst*. On Edward Street. Second storey added in 1902. Later owned by Mrs. Frank (Jura) Hall, Berkeley, California. Purchased in 1961 by Mr. and Mrs. E.W.T. Gill.

23. MacLaren, Miss Christina and Miss Roberta (Tina and Berta); Saint John. On Edward Street. One of the original owners was Sheriff Stuart. Later owned by Mrs. George Hooper, Ottawa (niece of the Misses MacLaren).

24. Shuter, Mr. and Mrs. George; Montreal (c. 1880). At Edward and Prince of Wales streets. Original owner was the Rev. A. MacLean, first regular minister at Greenock Church. Later owned by Judge Cockburn; Mr. and Mrs. Shuter; Mrs. Ann Rigby, St. Andrews.

25. Smith, E. Atherton; Saint John (1911). 60 Queen Street. Later owned by Dr John and Mrs. Hart; Dr. and Mrs. J. McLaughlin. Purchased in 1988 by Mr. and Mrs. James W. Eagles.

26. Thorp, Harry; Montreal (1947). Architect: Ross Wiggs, Montreal. At the corner of Water and Adolphus Streets. Later owned by Mr. C.D. Fitzgerald; K.G. Laberge; Kenneth G. Waiwood.

27. Reed, Gordon; Montreal (1947). Architect: Gordon Reed. 69 Water Street. Later owned by Mr. and Mrs. Gordon T. Shirres; Mrs. Shelagh Robinson.

28. Sills, Dean Charles Morton. *Ifield Cottage*. On Parr Street. Original house owned by the Stone family. Later owned by Mr. and Mrs. H.B. Robinson. Purchased in 1960 by Mr. and Mrs. Herbert Holland.

29. Walker, Mrs. Edward C.; Walkerville, Ontario (1910). On Reed Avenue. Later owned by Mrs. and Mrs. Guy Murchie; the Hon. and Mrs. C.D. Howe; Mr. and Mrs. Robert Craig, formerly of Montreal.

30. Macklem, O.R. (1913). Architect: Edward Maxwell. On Reed Avenue. Land bought from the Rev. Bowser on March 19, 1912. Later owned by Mr. L.O.P. Walsh, Montreal. Verandahs removed in 1961. Purchased 1961 by the Sir James Dunn Arena.

31. Guthrie, Norman G.; Ottawa (1924-1925). *Croix Crest*. On Mary Street. The Guthries' original house had been on the corner of Mary and Water streets and was torn down. Later owned by Mrs. Ralph Smith, Waterbury, Connecticut; Mr. and Mrs. Douglas Robinson.

32. Topp, Mr. and Mrs. W.H.; Montreal (c. 1854). 44 Water Street. Later owned by Mrs. A.W. Summerhill, Montreal, the daughter of Mr. and Mrs. W.H. Topp, a summer resident of the town for seventy-seven years. This house was in the Topp family for 109 years. Purchased in 1988 by Mrs. Lois Dack, Toronto.

33. Marshall, Thomas; Pittsburgh Pennsylvania. On Joe's Point Road. Original small house remodelled and placed next to Mr. Marshall's daughter's house (Mrs. Sarah Childs). Later owned by Mr. and Mrs. John T. Clark, Fredericton.

34. Childs, Mrs. Sarah. On Joe's Point Road. Originally owned by the Fryer and then the Halliday families. Later owned by Mr. and Mrs. Lyndon Dodge, New York, who enlarged it greatly (architect: Gordon Reed); Mrs. John F. Cundill, Ottawa. Purchased in 1988 by Mr. and Mrs. Harrison McCain and family, Florenceville, New Brunswick.

35. Russell, G. Horne (1924). Architect: Maxwell & Pitts. On Joe's Point Road. Later owned by Russell's son, Norman; Mr. and Mrs. Brian Devlin, Montreal, who converted it to an all-season residence; Dr. and Mrs. Alfred Needler.

36. Freeman, Halstead; New York (1947). Contractor: Wilfred Dalzell. *Tobermory*. On Joe's Point Road. Later owned by Mr. and Mrs. David Freeman and family, Rumson, New Jersey.

37. Magee, Col. Allan A.; Montreal (1943). Contractor: Wilfred Dalzell. The *Little House*. On Joe's Point Road. Sold in 1965 to Mr. and Mrs. T.R. Meighen and moved to the next lot. Main house built in 1967. Later owned by Senator Michael and Mrs. Kelly Meighen, Toronto.

38. Breese, William L.; Washington, D.C. (1942). Contractor: Wilfred Dalzell. On Joe's Point Road. Later owned by Mr. John Williamson, Fredericton.

39. Eidlitz, Ernest; New York (1962). On Joe's Point Road. This house was built down on the water at Hardings Point. Purchased in 1971 by Mr. and Mrs. William L. Breese and family, Washington, D.C.

40. Wainwright, Mrs. Arnold; Montreal (1850). On Joe's Point Road. Original house – the old Peacock house, formerly a farm – extended and renovated in 1920. Later owned by Mrs. Wainwright's sister, Miss Mona Prentice; Dr. and Mrs. Alfred Needler; Mr. and Mrs. G. Melvin Turner.

41. Christie, Katherine; Toronto (1950). *Wit's End*. On Joe's Point Road. An old

house was moved on to what was then C.P.R. land and a large room added. Later owned by Peter Pond. Destroyed by fire in 1980.

42. Tait, Sir Thomas (1928-1929). Architect: Edward Maxwell. *Linkscrest*. On Brandy Cove Road. Used as a convalescent home for R.C.A.F. and R.A.F. pilots during the Second World War. Later owned by Dr. and Mrs. Gavin Miller, Montreal; Dr. and Mrs. John Riddell; the Huntsman Marine Science Centre, for use as a residence.

43. Hume, Col. Frank; Houlton, Maine (1904). At Brandy Cove. Bought in 1916 by Fred P. McNichol of St. Stephen. Later owned by the latter's son, Frank McNichol; Mr. and Mrs. A.W. Guiness, Montreal; Mr. and Mrs. Douglas Ambridge, Toronto. The Huntsman Marine Science Centre presently operates on the site.

44. Bowser, the Rev. Alexander T.; U.S.A. (1898). *Cedar Croft*. On Cedar Lane. Later owned by Mr. and Mrs. C.T. Ballantyne, Montreal, who called the house *Bellenden*. Purchased in 1981 by Mr. and Mrs. H.B. Hodgson, formerly of Boston, Massachusetts.

45. Gordon, Blair; Montreal (1945). *Elbow Bend*. On Brandy Cove Road.

46. Huntsman, Dr. A.G.; Toronto (1950). 91 Cedar Lane. Dr. and Mrs. A.G. Huntsman converted the former Bowser hay barn into a charming house. Later owned by Dr. and Mrs. C.A. Mawson. Purchased 1982 by Mr. and Mrs. Heber Glenwright.

47. Hoar, Prof. Emery; Cambridge, Massachusetts (1885). On Mowat Drive. Prof. and Mrs. Hoar bought property on Humes Hill, now Mowat Drive, from Nathan Blakeney. Later owned by the Hon. C.D. Howe and Mrs. Howe; Dr. and Mrs. Reid A. Rawding; Capt. and Mrs. Norman Ryall (*Tara Manor Hotel and Restaurant*).

48. Tupper, Sir Charles; Nova Scotia and Ottawa (1872). *Highland Hill*. Three miles out on the Saint John Road. Land bought from Joseph Walton included a fine stone house built by Capt. Robert D. James. Later owned by Nathan Blakeney; Senator Robert Mackay; the Ralph Wilson Estate.

49. Mackay, Senator Robert; Montreal (1906). *Clibrig*. On the Saint John Road. The land and a stone house were purchased from Sir Charles Tupper in 1906. Later owned by Mr. and Mrs. Robert Loring, Montreal; Mr. Norman Wilson and Senator Cairine Wilson, Ottawa; Miss Cairine Wilson, St. Andrews.

Miss Cairine Wilson, daughter of Mr. Norman and Senator Cairine Wilson, tore down the old *Clibrig* and built a new house, *Clibrig II*, in 1973 on the same site; Architect: Stanley Emerson, Saint John. Houses on the site owned by Mr. Ralph Wilson, and by Gen. James and Mrs. Norma Davies.

50. Ross, Frank M. Upper Bayside, Highway No. 1. Originally built by John Mowat (Hurricane Jack) on an original grant of land to Mr. Robert Pagan and later to Dr. Calef. The house was extensively renovated after 1925. The main house later owned by Mr. and Mrs. John Norris, Montreal, and the lake house by the Rt. Hon. John Turner and Mrs. Turner, Toronto.

51. Shaughnessy, the Hon. Ann. *Innisfree*. At Bocabec, at the end of the Fiander Road overlooking the water. Ann Shaughnessy, youngest daughter of the second Lord and Lady Shaughnessy, rebuilt an old house on this site. Later owned by Lord and Lady Shaughnessy, London, England.

52. Ross, the Rev. H.P.; Plainsfield, New Jersey (1902). Architects: H.N. Black, Saint John and Eastport; Frank Adams, Providence, Rhode Island. *Rossmount*. When the Rev. and Mrs. Ross bought the Townsend house, they made many improvements and added a widow's walk. The house was destroyed by fire

in 1960. It was rebuilt and operated as the *Rossmount Hotel*.

53. Leighton, Delmar; Cambridge, Massachusetts (1934). Architect: Gordon Reed. *Beech Hill*. Mr. and Mrs. Leighton built their house next door to Dr. Grace Helen Mowat's *Beech Hill*, off Mowat Drive and overlooking the bay. They later called the new house *Beech Hill* and the Mowat house *Mowat Farm*.

54. Hope, William; Montreal (1901). Architect: Edward Maxwell. *Dalmeny*. Just above the railroad on the Bar Road. Destroyed by fire in 1946.

55. Hope, Charles; Montreal (1920-1925). At the end of the Bar Road just opposite the house of his father (William Hope). Former coachhouse on Prince of Wales Street, just opposite *The Fort*. Brought from the former Macklem-Walsh property next to the arena and converted to a summer house in 1962 by Mr. and Mrs. Charles Hope. Later owned by Robert Hope.

56. Maxwell, Edward; Montreal (1899). Architect: Edward Maxwell. *Tillietudlem*. On the Bar Road just below the railroad. Later owned by Mrs. Jean Fleming, the Maxwells' daughter; her son Maxwell Fleming; John Shaw; Mr. J.D. Gregorie, U.S.A.

57. Van Horne, Sir William; Montreal (1901). Designer: Sir William Van Horne. *Covenhoven*. Minister's Island. Minister's Island was purchased in 1891, but the house was not built until 1901. Later owners included a syndicate from Ohio in 1961; the New Englander Norman Langdon in 1971; Alexander George, Nova Scotia; Michael McPherson, Toronto. Purchased in 1982 by the Province of New Brunswick.

58. Knight, Miss Sarah Maria (1825). The *Anchorage*. Parr and Mary streets. Later owned by Mrs. Thomasina R. Andrews; Mr. and Mrs. Robert Gardiner Payne, New Jersey. Purchased in 1987 by Mr. and Mrs. Robert Stevens, Pennsylvania.

Index